DON'T GET FOOLED AGAIN

DON'T GET FOOLED AGAIN

The Sceptic's Guide to Life

Richard Wilson

ICON BOOKS

Published in the UK in 2008 by
Icon Books Ltd, The Old Dairy, Brook Road,
Thriplow, Cambridge SG8 7RG
email: info@iconbooks.co.uk

www.iconbooks.co.uk

Sold in the UK, Europe, South Africa and Asia
by Faber & Faber Ltd, 3 Queen Square,
London WC1N 3AU or their agents

Distributed in the UK, Europe, South Africa and Asia
by TBS Ltd, TBS Distribution Centre, Colchester Road,
Frating Green, Colchester CO7 7DW

This edition published in Australia in 2008
by Allen & Unwin Pty Ltd,
PO Box 8500, 83 Alexander Street,
Crows Nest, NSW 2065

Distributed in Canada by
Penguin Books Canada,
90 Eglinton Avenue East, Suite 700,
Toronto, Ontario M4P 2YE

ISBN: 978-184831-014-8

Text copyright © 2008 Richard Wilson

Typeset in Minion by Ellipsis Books Limited, Glasgow
Printed in the UK by Creative Print & Design, Blaina, Wales

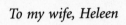

To my wife, Heleen

Richard Wilson read Philosophy at University College, London. His first book, *Titanic Express* (Continuum, 2006), recounts his search for the truth about the death of his sister Charlotte, who was killed in Burundi in 2000. He now works for a human rights organisation and lives in London with his wife, Heleen.

CONTENTS

CHAPTER ONE

'BECAUSE YOU'RE WORTH IT!'

The British are special, the world knows it, in our innermost thoughts, we know it. This is the greatest nation on Earth.

Tony Blair, prime minister of Great Britain[1]

It's a wonderful nation, the greatest on Earth. We think we're pretty good – and we are.

John Howard, prime minister of Australia[2]

Americans love being told we're the best, that we're number one. We will do anything – ANYTHING – to remain number one.

Frank Luntz, US Republican Party strategist[3]

Americans aren't alone in loving to be told that they're the best. As every salesman and Casanova knows, human beings the world over are more likely to give you what you want if you tell them how super-great they are while you're asking for it. Not only that, but across a range of different measures, most of us also believe that we are, if not the best, then certainly a whole lot better than most other people.

According to psychologists, the average person thinks that they're above average in terms of looks, intelligence, honesty, generosity, being a good friend, and taking the smaller bit of pizza when there are only two slices left.[4] We are more likely to remember our moments of glory, and more likely to forget our ignominious failures. We tend to think that the things we are bad at are things that most people are bad at, and that the things we are good at are rare and distinctive qualities.[5] In short, most of us seriously overrate ourselves, most of the time.

In everyday life, these delusions can be quite useful. Confident people tend to be more successful, and nothing boosts confidence more than the sure-fire conviction that you're smarter, friendlier, morally purer and more beautiful than the average bod. Optimists live longer,[6] get sick less often, are less likely to suffer heart disease[7] and – according to some studies – more likely to survive cancer.[8] Moreover, the people with the most accurate view of their own talents tend to be those with mental health problems. Research suggests that – contrary to popular belief – people who suffer from an eating disorder have a more realistic sense of their own level of attractiveness than those who don't,[9] and that clinical depressives are the group with the most consistently realistic view of their own abilities.[10] There's every reason to think that vanity is good for you, at least in small doses.[11]

The difficulty arises when our over-idealised view of ourselves collides violently with reality. The average driver thinks that they're better at driving than the average driver,[12] and at 80 mph in the dark on an icy road in the middle of winter this can cause serious problems. For the gambler on a losing streak in Las Vegas, or the happy recipient of an email informing the reader that he's been singled out to receive the long-lost fortune of a deceased third-world dictator, a dogmatic belief in one's own irrefutable special-ness can prove to be an expensive delusion.

This is a book about expensive delusions, and how to avoid them. It looks at the myriad ways in which we can deceive ourselves, and be deceived by others. We've all been fooled at one time or another – be it in love or in business, by the media or the promises of politicians. There are no solid guarantees that can protect us in future. But by learning more about the human weakness for wishful thinking, the mechanisms of psychological manipulation, the various forms in which delusion and deception can be manifested, and the tools that we can use to separate fact from fantasy, we can at least go some way towards inoculating ourselves.

Pigs and Pokes:
Don't get fooled by cockneys with megaphones

Sometime during the late 1980s, a buzz went up around my home town. The local paper had announced that a public auction was going to be held the following Saturday; Betamax videos, Amstrad computer games and all kinds of tempting consumer goods would be on offer at 'crazy, crazy prices'.

On the day of the sale, my best friend Jimmy and I joined the crowds cramming into the function room of the Salisbury Arms, pained at the 50p entrance fee, but confident of recouping our losses on the bargains we were going to snatch.

It all began modestly enough. A cockney with a megaphone at the front of the room wanted to know who would like to buy a tea towel for 2p, and flung them out to the lucky few who put their hands up quickly enough. Someone else in the crowd got a hairdryer for 15p. Another nabbed a food mixer for 20p, and then things really got going. He wasn't allowed just to *give* these things away, said the cockney with the megaphone, so we were going to play a little game. Who would offer him £5 for an empty box? For all we knew, he told us conspiratorially, it *could* just be an empty box ... but then it *might* contain one of the shiny new expensive things piled up in the display at the front of the room.

Laughing excitedly, one of my neighbours pulled out a £5 note and waved it in the air. Others followed, and soon the fivers were flying, as seemingly half the adult population of my town fell over themselves to hand in their cash for a 'pig in a poke'. And remember, said the man with the megaphone, don't open the box until you get home. That's all part of the fun.

The one-day-salers were long gone by the time the excitement had died down. At that point it became clear that there'd been a monumental rip-off. The £5 boxes contained nothing but worthless junk. The few people who had been given real consumer goods for a 'crazy, crazy price' appeared to have been stooges who were in on the scam.

The people of Hoddesdon, Hertfordshire had no grounds for legal redress. They'd been told that they were handing over their cash for something that might turn out to be worthless. The salesman had managed to fool the crowd completely, while speaking the literal truth. As grand deceptions go it was a fairly mild example, but for a wide-eyed teenager it was a still a useful lesson.

The scam worked by blinding the crowd to their better judgement, and pressurising them into making a rushed decision. The scammers got the crowd to 'decide in haste' by playing on their willingness to believe that there was a bargain to be had – but only if they could grab it before someone else got there. As many a salesman and fraudster knows, people are more likely to make a choice that they later regret if they're forced to make it in a hurry.

The mock auctions that toured southern England during my teenage years were merely the latest variation on an ancient con trick that was common across Europe during the Middle Ages. Dishonest market traders would sell bags or *pokes* (a word related to 'pocket'), and claim that the wriggling creature tied up in the bag was a young pig, when in fact it was one of little monetary value – typically a cat. The scam could be blown prematurely if someone 'let the cat out of the bag'. Nowadays, the phrase 'buying a pig in a poke' is a metaphor for any deal that involves paying for goods without seeing them upfront – or buying into an idea before giving it careful scrutiny.

Don't get fooled by your own propaganda

Being a sociable species, we tend to extend our convictions about ourselves to our nearest and dearest. If we are special, then so too are our children, our wider family, our friends, our football team and, of course, our country. In our innermost thoughts, every Briton knows – as does every American, Australian, Frenchman, Spaniard and Tongan – that the land of our birth is, without doubt, the greatest on the planet.

The flip side of thinking that we're not just special, but manifestly more special than other people, is that while we overrate ourselves and our own abilities, we typically underrate others. If Britain (or France or Australia or the USA) really is the greatest country on Earth, then it must follow that everyone else is second best.

At the extreme, our need to believe in our own superiority can leave us with a caricatured view both of ourselves and of those we see as outsiders – be that a group within our own society, or some foreign enemy. As we've seen many times throughout history, paranoid social divisions can easily be exploited by demagogues and conspiracy theorists. In the 1930s and '40s, the Nazis ruthlessly manipulated German fears of an international Zionist 'banking conspiracy' to justify the repression and extermination of millions of Jews, while the Soviets built a totalitarian regime around the terror of 'bourgeois counter-revolutionaries'. This can be dangerous not only to the demonised 'other', but also to one's own kind. The same hubris that led Hitler to think that his was a nation of supermen facing racially inferior opposition also led to his doomed attack on the USSR, based on the gloriously optimistic belief that 'we have only to kick in the door and the whole rotten structure will come crashing down'.[13]

Neither are well-established democracies immune from the dangers of hubris and grand delusion. Robert McNamara, who was US secretary of state for defence under Presidents Kennedy and Johnson during the 1960s, oversaw both the escalation of his country's involvement in Vietnam and the beginnings of the disaster that followed. His 576-page account of what went wrong makes for sobering reading.[14] McNamara argues that the American government failed because it overestimated its own military power, expected far too much of its weak and unpopular South Vietnamese allies, completely misunderstood the character and motivations of their North Vietnamese adversaries, and 'did not recognize that neither our people nor our leaders are omniscient'.[15]

'Hurrah for the Blackshirts!'

Over-idealising those we see as friends, allies or comrades can be just as damaging as caricaturing our enemies. At the very best, we risk making fools of ourselves – at the worst we leave ourselves vulnerable to the charge of moral complicity. Decades after the end of the Second World War, Britain's *Daily Mail* is still remembered for being the conservative newspaper that praised Adolf Hitler[16] and his British followers during the 1930s.[17] But we are less often reminded of the members of the political left who lined up during the same era to eulogise Stalin's Russia. The year before Lord Rothermere penned his famous piece cheering on Oswald Mosley's fascist Blackshirts, the eminent socialist George Bernard Shaw was writing to the *Guardian* to denounce media reports of slavery and mass starvation in the Soviet Union as a 'blind and reckless campaign'. In the midst of a man-made famine that ultimately claimed more than 3 million lives,[18] Shaw and his companions had been taken on an official tour of the USSR and found no evidence of what they believed were 'fantastic' lies and 'stale' slanders.[19] Shaw continued to defend the Soviet Union until the end of his life.[20]

One of the paradoxes of human nature is that the same species that has proved capable of such extremes of cruelty, selfishness and self-delusion has also, time and again, shown an enormous capacity for kindness, creativity and self-sacrifice. Another is that these two extremes so often exist side by side within the same person. Few, if any, people are wholly devoid of good qualities. The danger comes when we allow the good that we have found in someone to blind us to their darker side.

In the late 1970s, the American writer Norman Mailer

became closely involved with the case of Jack Abbott, a convicted killer, bank robber and forger.[21] Mailer had been so impressed by Abbott's writing abilities that he helped secure him a publishing deal and enthusiastically supported his application for parole, convinced that this talented writer was a changed man.[22] The resulting book, *In the Belly of the Beast*, was published to rave reviews in 1981. Abbott was freed in June of the same year, and quickly became the toast of the New York literary scene.[23] But just six weeks later, during a minor quarrel in a restaurant, he stabbed to death a 22-year-old waiter, Richard Adan. During the subsequent trial, Mailer urged that Abbott be treated leniently, suggesting that a long term in prison might stifle his creativity, and insisting that 'culture is worth a little risk'.[24] The actress Susan Sarandon, who also attended the trial, was so impressed by Jack Abbott that she named her son after him.[25] The court was less sympathetic, sentencing Abbott to fifteen years in jail. Mailer later admitted that his involvement with Abbott was 'a study in false vanity'.[26]

Many a criminal has enjoyed the support of well-meaning followers who simply cannot believe that the man they so admire could be capable of the depraved acts he stands accused of committing. Jack Abbott was, to Norman Mailer and many others, both a literary genius and an inspirational visionary; he was also a cold and impulsive killer. When they weren't engaging in robbery, extortion and murder, the cockney gangsters Ronnie and Reggie Kray were popular members of the London nightclub circuit who were famously 'good to their mother'.[27] Even Adolf Hitler, it is claimed, was tender and indulgent towards the children in his inner circle. Yet the evidence suggests that, even within a normal population, the line between saint and sadist may be perilously thin.

Men Behaving Badly –
The Stanford Prison Experiment

We want to believe we are good, we are different, we are better, or we are superior. But this body of social-psychological research ... shows that the majority of good, ordinary, normal people can be easily seduced, tempted, or initiated into behaving in ways that they say they never would.

Philip Zimbardo, psychologist, Stanford University[28]

In 1971, researchers at Stanford University set about recreating a prison environment in the psychology lab.[29] Twenty-four seemingly normal male student volunteers were randomly divided into two equal groups – half of them 'prisoners', and the other half 'guards'. Conditions were set to mirror real life as closely as possible. The experiment began when those selected as prisoners were arrested without warning by real police officers, taken from their homes, put through standard arrest procedures, and then transported to a set of prison cells in the basement of the Stanford University psychology department. On arrival they were sternly told that they had committed a crime, before being searched, stripped, deloused, assigned a number, shackled and put in a prison uniform.

The detainees were divided into groups and locked into four separate cells. For the duration of the experiment, they were referred to only by their prisoner numbers, and forced to cover their hair at all times. At regular intervals, including during the night, the prisoners would be taken from their cells and made to line up against the wall for an official inspection. Family visits were permitted, but were strictly controlled. Prisoners were allowed occasional meetings with a Catholic priest and a lawyer, both of whom behaved exactly as they would when visiting a real prison. Other than these procedures, the guards – who wore identical uniforms and mirrored sunglasses, and carried standard-issue billy-clubs – were given free rein to maintain order as they saw fit. The researchers secretly videotaped the results.

The guards reacted to their new-found power in three different ways. Some were indulgent, doing small favours for the prisoners and never punishing them. Some were 'tough but fair', simply following the guidelines that they had been given. But about a third of the guards showed clear sadistic tendencies, choosing to mete out arbitrary punishments for their own amusement, and constantly inventing new ways of humiliating their prisoners.

Punishments ranged from repeatedly forcing prisoners to do press-ups, placing them in solitary confinement and depriving them of their beds or blankets, to forcing them to clean the prison toilets with their bare hands, and forbidding them toilet access so that they had no choice but to urinate and defecate on the floor of their cells. As the experiment proceeded, the worst of the guards became increasingly brutal, and a number of prisoners began to show signs of extreme mental distress. The most sadistic and humiliating punishments happened at night, when the guards thought that no one else was watching. For ethical reasons, the researchers terminated the experiment after six days.

The Stanford prison experiment showed that even seemingly normal and well-balanced people can reveal sadistic tendencies when placed in a high-pressure environment, and given power over others. What we don't know – and are never likely to find out, because modern ethical controls would not allow the experiment to be repeated – is how far the guards would have gone if the study had not been terminated early.

Don't get fooled by the voice of authority

Between 1995 and 2004, an unknown man made a string of hoax phone calls to fast food outlets across the United States. The caller claimed to be a police officer investigating petty theft, and instructed store managers to carry out humiliating strip searches of their female workers. In the most extreme case, in Kentucky in 2004, a McDonald's manager named Donna Summers, together with her fiancé, detained an 18-year-old employee for more than three hours, during which time the girl was forced to perform a series of increasingly bizarre sexual acts. 'I honestly thought he was a police officer', Summers later insisted. 'I thought I was doing what I was supposed to be doing'.[30]

An experiment carried out by the psychologist Stanley Milgram in 1961 showed the startling extent to which we can be manipulated by those we perceive as figures of authority. Volunteers were told that they were involved in a study of learning and memory, with one participant playing the 'teacher' and the other the 'learner'. The teacher was to guide the learner through a series of memory tests. Every time the learner got a question wrong, the teacher was to administer an electric shock, with the voltage being progressively increased on each occasion, up to a maximum level of 450 volts.[31]

The process was overseen by a stern scientist wearing a white lab coat. If the teacher showed any hesitation in applying the electric shock, the scientist insisted that the learner would not suffer permanent health damage, and that the teacher had no choice but to continue. By 150 volts, the learner would be shouting with pain and saying that he refused to continue with the experiment. By 300, he would be complaining of a heart condition. Beyond 330, he would become completely silent.[32]

In reality, the selection process had been rigged, with

the 'learner' being played by an actor who was only feigning the effects of electrocution. The experiment's real purpose was to test how far the 'teachers' would go before they refused to administer an electric shock. Milgram's experiment had been explicitly designed, in the wake of the 1961 trial of the Nazi bureaucrat Adolf Eichmann, to simulate the systems of control used to induce thousands of ordinary Germans to participate in the extermination of Jews during the Second World War. Milgram and his colleagues had anticipated that less than 4 per cent of the volunteers would agree to continue beyond 300 volts. In fact, nearly three-quarters went beyond that level, while 60 per cent obeyed every order they were given, right up to the maximum voltage.[33]

The experiment worked by morally distancing the participants from the consequences of their actions. The subjects were addressed at all times as 'teacher', rather than by their real names, thus reinforcing the sense that they were functionaries performing an assigned role, rather than people making individual moral choices. Just as in Nazi Germany, subjects were induced to co-operate, in part, because the cruelty they were asked to inflict was initially quite mild, with the severity increasing in a series of small steps, each of them only marginally worse than the last.

If the teacher protested, the scientist would insist that he, not they, would be responsible for any harm that might be suffered by the learner, and instruct them forcefully to continue. And although the teacher could hear the learner's screams, the latter was hidden behind a partition screen. Subsequent experiments found that when this barrier was taken away – and especially when the teacher was required to force the learner's hand onto the electric plate in order to receive the shock – the compliance rate dropped significantly, although even under these conditions 30 per cent continued to cooperate. Milgram's results, which were replicated in similar tests that were carried out in Italy, Germany, South Africa and Australia, suggested that the psychology which enabled mass killing under the Nazis was by no means unique to that era.[34]

Why be a sceptic?

Looking at the history of our species, it's hard to believe that things would have gone better if people had asked fewer questions, and put more trust in cockneys with megaphones. From Khmer Rouge Cambodia to the Spanish Inquisition, humanity has a long and proud history of meekly engaging in depraved acts of inhumanity on the basis of ideas that, on closer examination, have turned out to be total gibberish. Nonsense has a lot to answer for.

Being human involves an odd dichotomy: we need to delude ourselves that we are exceptional, even if we aren't, in order to make the most of whatever potential we do have. We thrive on being told how great we are, and we gravitate towards people who are willing to indulge that need. It suits us, likewise, to lavish praise on those we love, respect or admire, and to turn a blind eye to their short-comings. Yet if we allow ourselves too much self-delusion, we are in danger of becoming fantasists, wide open to exploitation. And if we are too blind to the flaws of our heroes and idols – and too trusting of those we perceive to be figures of authority – we risk becoming complicit in the actions of criminals or, at the very least, making idiots of ourselves.

The good news from the psychologists is that we aren't wholly at the mercy of our raging egos. While most of us are heavily biased in favour of ourselves and our buddies, there are ways of minimising that bias when we need to. The antidotes to delusion are logic and evidence, prefer-ably evidence from multiple sources. We tend to delude ourselves least about the things that are easiest to measure objectively: the average person considers themselves to be exceptional in terms of warmth, honesty and generosity, but only slightly above average in intelligence. Some psychologists dub this – perhaps a little unfairly – the 'Mohammed Ali effect'; when asked in an interview whether he had failed the US army entrance exam on purpose, Ali's response was that 'I only said I was the greatest, not the smartest'.[35] Even the world's undisputed heavyweight egotist knew that he wasn't brilliant at everything.

Everyone is a sceptic to some degree, and the basis of scepticism is essentially common sense. Mohammed Ali knew that he wasn't the sharpest tool in the box because he'd been confronted with several bits of evidence – his consistent D-grade average at school, together with his failure to pass the army entrance exam – and it was an easy admission for him to make because he had plenty of other reasons to feel proud.

To be sceptical is to look closely at the evidence for a particular belief or idea, and to check for things that don't add up. Where possible, sceptics try to compare the evidence they have against information from alternative sources, and to look for inconsistencies and contradictions. This is not the same thing as being a cynic. Cynics like to assume the worst of people and things. Sceptics try to make as few assumptions as possible.

Yet neither does being a sceptic necessarily mean believing in nothing. There's no way to be sure, for example, that the world we see before us isn't a gigantic illusion – that we aren't all brains in vats wired up to some Matrix-like computer, our every thought and feeling controlled by deranged baby-eating evil genius alien lizard scientists. But unless we take it as a working assumption that this isn't the case, and that what we see and feel actually does correspond to something real, it can be difficult to get beyond the contents of our own heads.

It's all relative!

Some years ago, I got talking to a lawyer at a meeting of a UK parliamentary group looking at human rights in central Africa. When he asked what I was doing there, I told him about my sister, who had died while working in the region a couple of years earlier. I told him that I was trying to find out as much as I could about the circumstances of her death.[36] His response threw me: 'But do you think there really *is* such a thing as the truth about what happened?'

I'd come across this kind of relativistic thinking before. But it struck me that post-modern chic must have put down quite some roots in our culture when it can seem acceptable, in polite conversation, to suggest to the brother of a terror victim that there is actually no truth to know about his sister's death. While the glib catchphrase 'it's all relative' has become part of the currency of modern life, it's an idea with troubling implications. If all beliefs are equally valid, then what basis do we have for valuing the testimony of an Auschwitz survivor over that of a revisionist historian who denies that the holocaust ever took place? Or for believing the health claims of cancer researchers over those of a tobacco company? Or for thinking that two plus two equals four, rather than seven?

The paradox is that when scepticism collapses into relativism, we open the door to believing in anything and everything. If there's no such thing as truth, then there isn't much point in worrying whether or not your beliefs are truthful. If truth is entirely subjective, then it's futile even discussing your point of view with people you disagree with. If we reject logic, then it's impossible to put together any kind of system for distinguishing good ideas from gibberish.

We live in a sceptical age, and yet all kinds of outlandish beliefs – from astrology to grand global conspiracy theories – now seem increasingly mainstream. Some are no doubt quite harmless, others potentially deadly. Many more lie somewhere in the middle – they won't necessarily kill us, but they can leave us open to cynical manipulation. Newspaper headlines scream of the mortal threats that we face from mutant viruses, speed cameras and hydrogenated vegetable oil. A plethora of books, magazines and websites sell us 1,001 ways to 'discover the inner you', lose weight and find our perfect partner. There is no shortage of people promising to navigate us through life's pitfalls, from the smiling Scientologists offering 'free personality testing' on Tottenham Court Road to the friendly financiers suggesting we 'consolidate all our existing loans into one easy monthly payment'. Sweet-talking politicians promise a 'better deal for hard-working families'. Wide-eyed men in sandwich boards tell us that it's all the fault of the Israelis.

But while the jargon may change, many of these characters would have been familiar to the Ancient Greeks over 2,000 years ago. In fiercely competitive Athens, teachers of rhetoric, known as 'sophists', could command high fees. Some claimed to be able to teach wisdom and virtue. Others were more practical. 'Rhetoric is the only area of expertise you need to learn. You can ignore all the rest and still get the better of the professionals!' claimed the sophist Gorgias,[37] in words that wouldn't look out of place on the website of a modern-day self-help guru. The relativist's refrain that 'man is the measure of all things' was coined by another sophist, Protagoras, who was a contemporary of Socrates. In responding to him, Plato and Socrates helped to found the basis of modern philosophy and science. The word *sophistry* is now synonymous with fallacious arguments that are superficially plausible.

Logic, evidence and multiple sources

Socrates' method was to ask a series of questions, and then look for inconsistencies in the answers that he was given. This process of seeking out contradictions is an essential tool for all those whose job it is to separate truth from falsehood – from criminal investigators to journalists, historians and scientific researchers.

It's vital, too, that we are able to look closely at the evidence. If there were a patron saint of sceptics, it would surely be 'Doubting Thomas', the biblical disciple who appears in John's Gospel questioning the resurrection of Jesus. In the story, Thomas remains unconvinced until he's had a chance to see his master in the flesh and examine his wounds. Jesus then mildly chastises his doubting follower: 'Thomas, because thou hast seen me, thou hast believed: blessed are they that have not seen, and yet have believed.'[38]

We don't have to accept the literal truth of the story to feel some sympathy for St Thomas, who has had a fairly bad rap from Christians down the ages. His fellow disciples – presumably still traumatised by the brutal killing of their friend and master – had presented him with an outlandish tale about a man returning from the dead. Thomas just wanted to check out the evidence. Those 'who have not seen, and yet have believed' may be blessed, but they are also at risk of getting scammed, as my fellow townsfolk discovered in the late 1980s.

Sometimes, however, just seeing the evidence isn't enough. The presence of a walking, talking person who looks identical to someone previously thought dead would usually be taken as proof that that person is not dead after all – but other kinds of physical evidence need more scrutiny. In 1983, the German magazine *Stern* caused an international sensation when it announced the discovery of Adolf Hitler's diaries, and published detailed extracts. The *Sunday Times* snapped up the UK serialisation rights for thousands of pounds, and other newspapers and magazines around the world followed suit.[39] Historian Hugh Trevor-Roper set to work examining the diaries and declared them to be authentic, but many soon expressed scepticism. Graphologists noticed inconsistencies between the handwriting in the journals and known examples of Hitler's work. The very existence of the diaries seemed to contradict statements by the Führer's personal aides that he rarely wrote anything himself, preferring instead to dictate to an assistant. One entry was dated 20 July 1944, the day that Hitler had been injured in a bomb attack that severely limited the use of his arms – and, presumably, his ability to write.[40] The final blow was dealt when forensic examinations revealed that the diaries had been made using modern ink and paper – it was physically impossible that they could have been written during Hitler's lifetime.[41]

When historians evaluate a newly discovered document, they look to see how well it fits with what we already know. Suspicions about the 'Hitler diaries' began with the fact that they seemed to contradict so much of the accepted historical evidence. It was possible, at least in theory, that the accepted evidence, rather than the diaries, was false. But given the volume of material that would have to have been discounted if the diaries were to be accepted as genuine – from the personal testimonies of those who had known Hitler to the established facts about ink and paper production in the 1930s – the hypothesis that the diaries had been faked seemed far more plausible. There was, in other words, a coherent alternative explanation of the diaries' existence, which seemed to fit the accumulated facts better than the claim that these were the authentic diaries of Adolf Hitler.

There were also clear vested interests at stake. Gerd Heidemann, the German journalist who originally presented the diaries to the world, was not a neutral observer. He had already been paid good money for the story, so he had a great deal to gain from the diaries being accepted as genuine. It also later emerged that Hugh Trevor-Roper, one of the historians who had authenticated the diaries, had a financial stake in the *Sunday Times* which had paid so much money for the right to publish them. This conflict of interest raised doubts about Trevor-Roper's status as a truly independent expert.

But perhaps most dangerous of all was the fact that, from the moment the diaries' existence was revealed, newspaper editors were under enormous pressure to make a rushed decision. Had the diaries turned out to be genuine, the *Sunday Times* would have pulled off one of the scoops of the century. But just like the victims of a mock auction who fear missing out on a bargain if they don't hand over their fivers quickly enough, the editors knew that someone else might well snap up the exclusive publishing rights if they didn't get there first. This created a strong incentive to cut corners, and to rush through the time-consuming checks that might otherwise have detected the hoax early on. Within days of declaring himself satisfied of the diaries' authenticity, the historian Hugh Trevor-Roper was expressing doubts – but by then it was too late. His reputation, and that of the *Sunday Times*, suffered lasting damage. The Hitler diaries quickly went from being evidence in a historical investigation to being evidence in a criminal trial. The journalist Gerd Heidemann and the forger who had worked with him were each prosecuted and sentenced to 42 months in jail.[42]

Another crucial tool for detecting tomfoolery is the use of multiple sources. In December 2006, the French-language Belgian state broadcaster *Radio Télévision Belge de la Communauté Française* (RTBF) ran a spoof news feature claiming that the Dutch-speaking region of Flanders had declared independence, effectively abolishing Belgium.[43] The programme showed pictures of cheering crowds waving the Flemish flag, and claimed that trams and buses were now being stopped at the linguistic border. Among the thousands fooled were, reportedly, a number of foreign diplomats, who began cabling urgent communications to their home governments.[44] Had they taken the trouble, as many sceptical Belgians did, to check what other news sources were saying, they would quickly have realised that RTBF was the only channel reporting the alleged break-up of the nation. All other stations – including every Flemish-language broadcaster – were continuing their programmes as normal.

It makes sense to check alternative sources because while, on occasions, one trusted news outlet may be duped – or persuaded to run a satirical hoax – it's far more difficult, in a democratic society, to get every journalist in the nation to play along. And yet there are still many occasions when large sections of the press are deceived – and end up deceiving us. The next chapter will look at the evasions and manipulations of the PR industry.

CHAPTER TWO

DON'T GET FOOLED
BY PSEUDO-NEWS

In October 1990, a fifteen-year-old Kuwaiti girl testified before the United States Congress about the atrocities she had witnessed in her country, which was then under Iraqi occupation. 'Nurse Nayirah' was tearful as she described how Iraqi soldiers had broken into Kuwait City's Al-Adan hospital, removed children from their incubators, stolen the machines, and 'left the babies on the cold floor to die'.[1]

Nayirah's account caused outrage around the world, and hardened congressional support for a war to free Kuwait, at a time when opinion had been wavering. Amnesty International cited Nayirah's claims in a report on the Iraqi occupation, and suggested that more than 300 babies had died.[2] The US government repeated the allegations several times in the run-up to the January 1991 congressional vote on military action.[3] In the end, the motion was passed by a margin of just five votes – with seven members citing the incubator story as a factor in their decision to support war.[4]

But soon after the conflict was over, serious questions began to be raised. Staff at the Al-Adan hospital denied that the incident had ever happened – or that Nayirah had even worked there. Amnesty issued a retraction, having found no credible evidence for the incubator claims.[5] The human rights group Middle East Watch, after carrying out an investigation of their own, reportedly denounced Nayirah's allegations as a 'complete hoax'.[6] There had been some atrocities, but the headline-grabbing, vote-swinging incubator story could not be substantiated.

It only emerged later that 'Nurse Nayirah', who'd supposedly been unable to reveal her full name for security reasons, was the daughter of Kuwait's ambassador to the United States,[7] and a member of the Kuwaiti royal family, whose autocratic rule the Iraqi invasion had overthrown.[8] Before giving her testimony, Nayirah had been coached by the PR firm Hill and Knowlton, which had been paid several million dollars by the Kuwaiti government-in-exile – via a front group, 'Citizens for a Free Kuwait' – to make the case for war.[9]

The Kuwait contract was reportedly Hill and Knowlton's largest to date,[10] with more than 100 staff employed in twelve offices across the US.[11] Between the Iraqi invasion of August 1990 and the congressional vote of January 1991, Hill and Knowlton had lobbied newspaper editors, organised press conferences and rallies, arranged media interviews and produced dozens of 'video news releases'[12] for distribution to TV stations around the world. Often these were simply incorporated into news reports, with no mention of who had funded their production. Tens of thousands of 'Free Kuwait' T-shirts and bumper stickers were distributed across US universities on behalf of 'Citizens for a Free Kuwait',[13] again with no indication that these had been paid for by the Kuwaiti authorities. Of the $12 million donated to 'Citizens for a Free Kuwait', $11.9 million came from Kuwait's government. Just $17,861 came from private donations.[14]

Public opinion was monitored by Hill and Knowlton's research arm, the Wirthlin Group, to identify the messages that the American public found most persuasive. Wirthlin even surveyed TV audiences on changes to the Kuwaiti ambassador's hairstyle and clothing that might make him seem more likeable.[15] Hill and Knowlton's efforts – and in particular the 'Nurse Nayirah' story – have been credited with swinging the balance of opinion, both in Congress and among the American public, in favour of military action.

Looking again at the video footage of 'Nurse Nayirah', it seems understandable that her testimony was taken at face value. Even a hardened hack might find it difficult to be cynical about the words of a tearful fifteen-year-old girl. Nayirah's reason for not revealing her full name at least seemed credible at the time. The very fact that her country was under occupation meant that journalists could not go and verify the claims for themselves. And while the baby-incubator claim carried particular emotional resonance, it was not so different in character from other substantiated abuse allegations.

But the fact remains that the public – both in the US

and worldwide – had been sold a 'pig in a poke'. As a member of the Kuwaiti royal family, Nayirah had a vested interest in provoking a US-led invasion. And as the young daughter of her country's ambassador she may also have been particularly vulnerable to manipulation. Even if we take the most charitable view possible of the fact that her identity was withheld, it's difficult to see what could justify disguising the fact that 'Citizens for a Free Kuwait', the ostensibly independent campaign which accompanied her testimony, was funded almost entirely by the Kuwaiti government.

The story of 'Nurse Nayirah' has since come to acquire totemic significance among critics of the PR industry. For some, it seems to be the clearest possible illustration of the extent to which grave government decisions can be manipulated by spin and fabrication. In an article published in February 2002, the United Press International news agency reported asking Hill and Knowlton 'if it now acknowledges the incubator story as a deception':

> 'The company has nothing to say on this matter,' media liaison Suzanne Laurita replied. When asked if such a deception would be considered part of the public relations business, she answered: 'Please know again that this falls into the realm that the agency has no wish to confirm, deny or comment on.'[16]

Lauri Fitz-Pegado, the Hill and Knowlton staffer who

oversaw the 'Nayirah' hearing, continues to deny that the story was fabricated. In a 2003 interview, Fitz-Pegado claimed that a Kuwaiti-commissioned 1991 report by the Kroll Associates firm of private investigators had substantiated Nayirah's allegations, and that it was available to anyone who wanted to read it.[17] But when contacted, Kroll Associates were unable to provide a copy. Neither the Kuwaiti government nor Lauri Fitz-Pegado responded to my enquiries. Others who were involved at the time, notably Brent Scowcroft, the former presidential National Security Adviser, have said publicly that they now believe the allegations were untrue.[18]

One of the central tenets of news is that a journalist always protects the anonymity of his or her sources. But this means that the public must rely wholly on the journalist to ensure that those sources are credible. Even when a source is named, we will usually have only the briefest of information about who they are. Did they come to the journalist independently, or were they put forward by someone with a vested interest in promoting a particular version of events? Is the journalist themselves fully aware of their source's background and motivations? Did the story start with a government leak, an anonymous email, a press conference or a phone call from some special interest group? Were they immediately convinced that the issue was worth covering, or did they have to be charmed into running the story by a sweet-talking public relations executive?

'Where once journalists were active gatherers of news, now they have generally become mere passive processors of unchecked, second-hand material', argues the veteran reporter Nick Davies.[19] For his detailed investigation of the modern media, *Flat Earth News*, Davies commissioned a study into 2,000 reports from *The Times*, *Telegraph*, *Guardian* and *Independent* newspapers. In only 12 per cent of cases was there clear evidence that the facts in the story had been thoroughly checked before publication. Researchers found that 80 per cent had been 'wholly, mainly or partially constructed from second-hand material, provided by news agencies and by the public relations industry'.

In the UK alone, there are 48,000 people working in the PR industry[20] – people whose main purpose is to persuade journalists to report the news in a way that favours the interests of their employers.[21] PR professionals talk of 'selling in' a story to journalists. And just as sales reps are judged by the brutal bottom line, so PR executives are assessed by the coverage that they can secure. According to the latest available research, £6.5 billion is spent on PR in Britain every year.[22] Worldwide, the figure has been estimated to be as high as £100 billion.[23]

CHAPTER THREE

THE SMOKING–CANCER 'CONTROVERSY'

Viewed from any perspective, the record of the PR firm Hill and Knowlton seems extraordinary. During the early 1990s, at the same time as it provoked international outrage over atrocities in Kuwait, Hill and Knowlton was working to defend the Indonesian government over its brutal occupation of East Timor.[1] Among the company's more controversial clients have been the infamous Bank of Credit and Commerce International (BCCI),[2] Enron,[3] the Catholic Church[4] and the Church of Scientology,[5] together with the governments of Turkey, Angola, Peru, Egypt,[6] Botswana,[7] Uganda[8] and the Maldives.[9] Just a few years before the Kuwait controversy, the firm was hired to advise the Chinese communist government after the Tiananmen Square massacre.[10] In the early 1990s, a Hill and Knowlton executive was said to have boasted that 'we'd represent Satan if he paid'.[11]

But perhaps Hill and Knowlton's most stunning success was its role in defending the tobacco industry against claims that cigarettes were to blame for the huge rise in lung cancers during the first part of the 20th century. Few scientific controversies have ever been as fiercely contested, and few settled quite so conclusively. It is now almost universally accepted that smoking is a major cause of cancer – but until the 1970s, the tobacco industry fought a sustained campaign to convince the public that the case remained unproven. From cutting-edge public relations techniques to attempts to co-opt reputable scientists, from the 1950s onwards every conceivable tool was employed to shape the scientific debate and – even more crucially – to shape the way that this debate was presented in the mainstream media.[12]

Concerns about a link between cigarettes and cancer were being raised as early as the late 1920s, when it was already clear that the rise in cigarette consumption from the beginning of the 20th century had been accompanied by a huge increase in lung cancer.[13] But it was only several decades later that a clear scientific consensus began to emerge. From 1950 onwards, a series of studies showed that those who smoked were overwhelmingly more likely to develop cancer than those who didn't.[14] Although the precise mechanism was still unknown, as the decade progressed a clear majority of cancer scientists began to be convinced of a causal link.[15]

'No public relations expert has ever been handed so real and yet so *delicate* a multi-million dollar problem,'[16] wrote T.V. Hartnett, president of the cigarette firm Brown and Williamson, following an industry-wide crisis conference in December 1953. Soon afterwards, tobacco executives agreed to hire Hill and Knowlton, the leading public relations firm of its time. The company's co-founder, John Hill, took personal charge of the account.[17]

The strategy that Hill recommended was not to deny outright that cigarettes caused cancer, but to insist that the case was 'not proven'. The public had to be convinced that there were 'two sides' to the story.[18]

The campaign began on 4 January 1954 with the publication of the tobacco industry's 'Frank Statement To Cigarette Smokers', which appeared in 448 newspapers in 258 cities across the US:

> Recent reports on experiments with mice have given wide publicity to a theory that cigarette smoking is in some way linked with lung cancer in human beings.
>
> Although conducted by doctors of professional standing, these experiments are not regarded as conclusive in the field of cancer research. However, we do not believe that any serious medical research, even though its results are inconclusive, should be disregarded or lightly dismissed
>
> At the same time, we feel it is in the public interest to call attention to the fact that eminent doctors and research scientists have publicly questioned the claimed significance of these experiments.[19]

Clearly *some* scientists now believed that tobacco did pose serious risks, but others disagreed. More research was needed in order to establish the facts – a noble aim to which, of course, the industry was fully committed. To this end, cigarette companies announced the creation of the Tobacco Industry Research Committee (TIRC):

> In charge of the research activities of the Committee will be a scientist of unimpeachable integrity and national repute. In addition there will be an Advisory Board of scientists disinterested in the cigarette industry. A group of distinguished men from medicine, science, and education will be invited to serve on this Board. These scientists will advise the Committee on its research activities.

In reality, as industry executives later admitted, the TIRC was largely a PR operation. In a 1988 court case, Judge H. Lee Sarokin concluded that the committee was 'nothing but a hoax created for public relations purposes with no intention of ever seeking the truth or publishing it'.[20]

The 'scientist of unimpeachable integrity' selected to chair the TIRC was Clarence Cook Little, a geneticist who had worked with the prestigious American Society for the Control of Cancer. But despite his track record, Little was anything but 'disinterested'. Confidential records of an early TIRC meeting reveal Little's view that the tobacco industry had been under 'attack' for 200 years, and that the main purpose of the TIRC was 'to build a foundation of research sufficiently strong to arrest continuing or future attacks'.[21] Far from being an objective and impartial search for the truth, the TIRC's work was focused from the start on winning a political battle for the tobacco industry.

It was a fight that Clarence Cook Little relished. Throughout his career, he had been drawn to controversy and confrontation, taking a provocative stance on issues ranging from birth control to eugenics.[22] A self-declared 'ultraconservative about cause and effect',[23] Little had worked in medical science since the 1920s, when research was still heavily shaped by the theories and methods of the 19th century. Like many of his era, Little was deeply suspicious of the use of statistics and clinical data. The major medical breakthroughs of his youth had come not through number-crunching but through the individual toil of lone laboratory researchers like Louis Pasteur. Little was convinced that the solution to the cancer 'mystery' would be found in the same way.[24] Even more importantly, perhaps, as a lifelong eugenicist and genetics researcher, Clarence Cook Little was deeply committed to the belief that major dysfunctions of the body, such as cancer, must ultimately have a hereditary cause rather than an environmental one.[25]

Little's objection to the statistical studies was less about the detail, and more about the very definition of the word 'cause'. For Little, a cause had to be something you could demonstrate under laboratory conditions. It was not enough to show that the overwhelming majority of lung cancer victims were smokers, however high the figures and however strong the correlation. For a cause to be proven, Little insisted, researchers would need to explain the precise mechanism at work, just as the heroes of the 19th century had done.[26]

In an exchange with Little published in 1961 in the *New England Journal of Medicine*, the cancer researcher Ernst Wynder expressed the frustration felt by many within the scientific community:

> I know of no other chronic disease that has been studied epidemiologically and statistically in such detail and with such uniform results as smoking and lung cancer … Of those who will not accept existing evidence, I should like to know what evidence would be acceptable. If one criticizes epidemiology for being statistical, if one criticizes animal research for being unrelated to the human problem and if one criticizes chemical identification of carcinogens as not having any bearing to human disease, I should like to ask if there is a form of evidence that would be accepted as being conclusive. If it were humanly possible we would at once set up a study that could yield such evidence. If it is humanly impossible, it is not a constructive kind of suggestion that would advance scientific knowledge.[27]

Clarence Cook Little refused to give an answer, insisting that 'if one could define such specific evidence the problem would already be solved.'[28]

In other ways, Little's 'scepticism' about the smoking–cancer link was less philosophical and more obviously partisan. As a young scientist, the TIRC chairman had pioneered the use of inbred laboratory mice in medical research.[29] But now, as a series of such tests seemed to show that exposure to cigarette smoke could trigger lung cancer in mice, he sought to downplay the value of animal testing – except in cases where the results seemed favourable to the tobacco industry.

'When possible,' noted one industry review in the 1970s, 'Dr Little qualifies the results of animal tests that tend to be critical, but emphasises them when they do not find evidence of carcinoma, implying that smoking is harmless. The aim of his summations, all too apparently, seems to be to protect smoking.'[30]

While the industry was keen to highlight the amount it spent on 'research',[31] much of the TIRC's money was actually used for advertising and PR, rather than science. The studies that it did fund were focused on everything but the basic question the committee had ostensibly been established to resolve – whether or not smoking caused cancer.[32] Clarence Cook Little rejected any idea of doing research on the composition of cigarette smoke. That would be a waste of time, he insisted, as smoke had never been shown to be carcinogenic. Animal experiments – and of course statistical studies – were also ruled out. After initial research looked in vain for some other factor to explain the rise in lung cancer, the TIRC contented itself with highly technical studies, focusing on the development of cancer rather than its cause[33] – all the while repeating the mantra that 'more research is needed'.

Even as Little's reputation among his fellow scientists diminished,[34] Hill and Knowlton worked to promote him as a leading authority ready to comment on, and downplay, each new piece of research that pointed to a link between smoking and cancer.[35] Those who raised concerns about the health effects of smoking were dismissed not in scientific but political terms, as 'anti-tobacco propagandists'.[36] According to one Hill and Knowlton executive, Carl Thompson:

> One policy that we have long followed is to let no major unwarranted attack go unanswered. And that we would make every effort to have an answer in the same day – not the next day or the next edition. This calls for knowing what is going to come out both in publications and in meetings.[37]

Hill and Knowlton played expertly on the media's penchant for reporting 'both sides of the story'.[38] Although Little represented an increasingly discredited and marginalised point of view among scientists,[39] Hill and Knowlton had great success in insisting that his comments be given equal weight to those of the independent cancer researchers who were actually studying the matter at hand.

Even as the evidence of a link between smoking and

cancer became overwhelming, Hill and Knowlton achieved continued success in persuading the public that the matter was still open to debate. 'From time to time, man-on-the-street interviews ask about the smoking question', reported a Hill and Knowlton memo in 1962. 'In almost every one of these, there will be a quotation that is almost an exact paraphrase of some statement issued for the tobacco accounts'.[40] This attitude was mirrored in cigarette sales, which continued to rise long after a comprehensive government investigation had concluded, in 1964, that smoking did indeed cause cancer. In the US, sales of cigarettes reached their peak in 1975, nearly a quarter of a century after the publication of the first studies suggesting a smoking–cancer link. Lung cancer rates continued to rise through to the mid-1990s.[41]

The genius of Hill and Knowlton's PR strategy was that it capitalised on one of the most profound facts about the working of the media – that 'debate' makes for a much more interesting story than consensus. An article that offers two conflicting views about a scientific study, and then leaves the conclusion open, will have far greater appeal for journalists – and their readers – than one that simply reports the results as fact. Controversy sells;[42] newspapers have a strong financial incentive to print stories that stir up arguments rather than settling them. In addition, 'controversy' is a vague and amorphous term. Strictly speaking, any issue where someone, somewhere, disputes the facts of the case can be deemed 'controversial' –

whatever the disputer's motivations, and however flawed their argument.

Smoking, cancer and pseudoscience

One of the tell-tale signs of pseudoscience is a double standard in the evaluation of evidence. When tests on mice and rats seemed to support the smoking–cancer hypothesis, Clarence Little would seek to question the very validity of animal experimentation as a research method. But when the studies found no evidence of a link between smoking and cancer, he would raise no such objections. Genuine scientists take a consistent approach to their research methods, rather than rejecting a method only when it yields results that they dislike.

Another characteristic feature is a demand for an unrealistically high standard of proof for the claim under discussion. No matter how much epidemiological data existed showing that smokers were overwhelmingly more likely to get cancer than non-smokers, or experimental data showing that smoke was carcinogenic in mice, Little insisted that the case was 'not proven' because scientists had not yet been able to show, in laboratory conditions, the precise mechanism by which the disease was triggered in humans. But more than this, he refused to discuss, even in theoretical terms, what a 'proof' of the smoking–cancer link could look like. This was essentially a political tactic. By refusing to agree to any possible set of conditions that would, should they be fulfilled, compel him to accept the smoking–cancer hypothesis, Clarence Cook Little was ensuring that he could never be caught out by the evidence.

Clarence Cook Little stuck resolutely to his 'ultraconservative' position right up until his death in 1971. Historians still debate the extent to which he was genuinely convinced by it. But there is no doubt that he, along with the small number of scientists who joined him at the Tobacco Industry Research Committee, proved enormously useful in efforts to maintain the illusion of controversy, and stave off political pressure for regulation.

By co-opting and corrupting a small section of the scientific community, and then investing an enormous amount of time and money into getting these marginalised voices heard in the media, the tobacco industry was able to amplify out of all proportion the true character and extent of scientific doubts about the link between smoking and cancer. By exploiting the inherent vagueness of such notions as 'consensus', and cleverly playing to the media's penchant for 'controversy', the TIRC was able to ensure that obscure and discredited objections to the smoking–cancer hypothesis were given far more prominence than they deserved.[43] Harvard historian Allan M. Brandt has described the tobacco industry's systematic deception over the health risks of smoking as the 'crime of the century',[44] contributing to tens of millions of premature deaths worldwide.

41

The PR methods developed by Hill and Knowlton became the blueprint for companies fighting a rearguard action against overwhelming scientific evidence. In 1983, the firm helped building materials company US Gypsum draw up a strategy to manage fears about the danger of asbestos, which had been used widely in its products until the late 1970s. Documents released during a subsequent court case show that Hill and Knowlton advised the company to set up an industry group to 'take the heat from the press and industry critics', and recruit scientists to act as 'independent experts' to argue that asbestos was safe.[45] The following year, the 'Asbestos Institute'[46] was established in Canada – the world's largest asbestos exporter – to 'promote the safe use of asbestos in Canada and throughout the world'.[47]

'The truth, as always, is somewhere in the middle'

In a democratic society, where compromise can be seen as tantamount to a civic duty, it is easy to assume that there are 'two sides to every story' – that, given any pair of opposing views, the truth will always be somewhere between them. The format of many TV, radio and newspaper reports tends to reinforce this mindset. A representative of one side will be invited to make a comment, and then an opposing view will be presented, with the reporter acting as a kind of referee. Even when a journalist isn't explicitly reminding us that 'the truth, as always, is somewhere in the middle',[48] the very fact that these two particular views have made it into the mainstream media automatically confers some degree of legitimacy on them both. And the fact that both are given equal airtime can add to the impression that they are both equally worthy of attention. From here, it's easy to slide into the conclusion that the truth must lie roughly halfway between the two viewpoints.

But if we take this principle too far, it can lead us into dangerous territory, and here the issue of 'selection bias' plays a vital role. The halfway point in a TV interview with a government minister on the issue of racism, for example, will look very different if the opposing view is from a human rights activist rather than a member of Migration Watch, or the British National Party. Similarly, the halfway point in an interview with the Archbishop of Canterbury will be very different if the counterpoint is from an atheist like Richard Dawkins rather than a Muslim imam. Even where the journalist conducting the discussion takes a meticulously balanced approach, the very choice of interviewees will inevitably constrain the debate and lead the audience in a particular direction.

And while it may be *polite* to treat all views as equally valid, if we are interested in getting to the truth, rather than simply building an agreeable consensus, we will need to take a more nuanced approach. At its worst, the 'somewhere in the middle' mindset can be strongly biased in favour of the status quo, pushing us towards a homogenised average of the views that manage to make their way into the media, however barmy, extreme or well-funded: Is homosexuality an abomination in the sight of God or simply a lifestyle choice? Was Princess Diana's death an accident or murder? Do cigarettes cause cancer or don't they? Did the Holocaust happen or didn't it? It's hard to argue that 'the truth is somewhere in the middle' in these cases. There comes a point at which, paradoxically, fence-sitting can become another variety of dogma.

CHAPTER FOUR

SELECTION BIAS –
THE HIDDEN MENACE

The slick production of a modern media report, and the authoritative air of those presenting it, can give a highly misleading impression of what 'news' actually amounts to. The stories being played out on our screens may seem to be a fair and balanced account of the most important things going on in the world, but they are, in reality, the product of an extremely selective process, tailored to appeal to a particular audience, tempered by the fear of litigation and subject, in most cases, to the constraints of a ruthlessly competitive market.

News coverage is slanted towards those stories that are cheap to research, attention-grabbing and straightforward to explain: a 'kiss and tell' celebrity sex scandal, a speech by a high-profile politician, the latest terror scare, or a story handed to the journalist on a plate by a PR agency. Issues that require time-consuming, expensive or dangerous research, and that can't easily be summarised in an appealing way, will inevitably be under-represented.

A British journalist seeking to report, for example, on the conflict in the Democratic Republic of Congo will first have to stump up the money to fly there, and then try to find a way of travelling round the country without falling victim to one of the many armed groups who prey on the population.[1] Even if this proves possible, unless he happens to be fluent in Kifulero or Swahili, he will have to work through local translators – and hope that witnesses will agree to speak openly – if he wants to gain any understanding of what local people are thinking. And even then, the difficulty of grasping, let alone explaining, the complexities of the situation will add an additional barrier. Faced with such problems, it seems understandable that the journalist might prefer to stay home and write about the latest news from *Celebrity Big Brother*.

This filtering process is sometimes called 'selection bias'. Even where a newspaper upholds the highest standards of accuracy and fairness in its reporting, the choice of which issues to report and which to ignore can itself create a distorted impression. The fact that our news-stands are filled with 'silent killers', 'deadly threats' and 'hidden menaces' reflects less the true scale of the dangers that we face, and more the extent to which fear sells papers.

Most of us have a fairly well-developed instinct for self-preservation, so any headline that warns of an immediate danger can have us reaching for our small change, or at least arouse some interest. But the result is that the media has a strong financial incentive to engage in fear mongering. Newspapers have become adept at seeking out potential threats – however obscure and unlikely – and presenting them to us as dramatically as possible.

In the strange parallel universe of tabloid journalism, one sensational murder close to home can receive far more coverage than a million deaths in a distant land, and the vaguest of rumours can make a front-page headline. Ruthless terror gangs plot to murder thousands by blowing up jumbo jets with cans of Fanta. Paedophile perverts lurk in every town, waiting to snatch our children from us and murder them live on the internet. Foreign plagues with strange acronyms infest our hospitals and threaten to wipe out our civilisation. While most of these threats are real at least in theory, the coverage they get can be very misleading. It doesn't help that human beings are consistently bad at calculating low probabilities. The same mental 'trick of the light' that makes us overestimate our chances of winning the lottery can also have us lying awake worrying about highly unlikely worst case scenarios.

But the truth is that our children are more likely to kill themselves than die at the hands of a random stranger. And the biggest threat of all is not hiding in the bushes in the park, but sitting behind the wheel of a car.[2] While the handful of children murdered by paedophiles every year regularly feature on the tabloid front pages, the dozens killed in road accidents are usually relegated to the local media – if they get a mention at all. Among adults, suicide is an even greater killer than car accidents – and far more deadly than terrorism. Based on current form, the average Briton is more of a threat to him or herself than is Osama bin Laden. In 2005, the year that saw 52 people killed in the worst-ever terror attack on UK soil,[3] a staggering 5,000 more committed suicide,[4] while twenty times that number are believed to have died of a smoking-related disease.[5] But these lonely, quiet de rigueur deaths have none of the dramatic impact of a random act of terror.

Cruder still, perhaps, is the extent to which commercial news is constrained by pressure from advertisers, or the business objectives of the media group's owners. The News Corporation, owned by the Australian-born media magnate Rupert Murdoch, has been criticised for muting criticisms of China, where Murdoch is working to expand his business. In 1993, Murdoch famously dropped the BBC World Service from his Asian satellite TV network, reportedly following complaints from the Chinese government about critical coverage.[6] Five years later, another Murdoch-owned company, HarperCollins, cancelled a book by former Hong Kong governor Chris Patten amid alleged fears that it would displease the Chinese authorities.[7]

In August 2000, a Florida court awarded $425,000 to Jane Akre, a former Fox News employee.[8] She and her fellow reporter, Steve Wilson, had been fired from a local TV station after refusing to include information they believed to be false in a news feature on the use of artificial hormones in milk production. The husband-and-wife team were investigating concerns that the use of these hormones, produced by the drug company Monsanto, could lead to health problems among the public, including an increased risk of cancer.[9] When Monsanto threatened legal action, the Fox network pulled the programme shortly before it was due to be broadcast.[10]

The case also raised a wider problem, caused by the size of both companies. Not only were Monsanto in a position to sue; as the manufacturer of a range of other products, including the leading artificial sweetener, Nutrasweet, they were also a major advertiser. Any boycott of the network by Monsanto could have hit Fox very hard financially, and affected 22 TV stations across the US.

A year of wrangling followed in which Monsanto, and representatives of the dairy industry, pressurised the TV station's management to edit the story to their satisfaction. Akre and Wilson agreed to a number of changes but refused to include information that they thought was untrue. When pressed, they threatened to report the station to the Federal Communications Commission (FCC) for attempting to falsify news. Eventually both journalists were fired.

Akre and Wilson sued under Florida's whistleblower legislation, which protects employees who refuse to break the law in the course of doing their job. While Wilson's case was unsuccessful, the court found in favour of his partner Jane Akre. But in 2003, Fox successfully appealed, after reportedly arguing that the falsification of news was not technically illegal.[11]

The Akre and Wilson case was not exceptional. In 2003, a survey of US business editors found that in the past year alone, 12 per cent had 'been asked to lie or soften a story that an advertiser might find objectionable'. Thirty per cent admitted succumbing to such pressure at some stage in their careers.[12] A global survey in 2007 found that 54 per cent of editors worldwide regarded shareholder or advertiser pressure as the greatest threat to their independence.[13]

But perhaps the murkiest area of 'pseudo-news' – and one that's always far easier to suspect than to prove – is the problem of undisclosed affiliations. In the USA in January 2005, it was revealed that two newspaper columnists, Michael McManus and Maggie Gallagher, had accepted thousands of dollars in covert payments from the US government in exchange for promoting Bush administration policies in their newspaper columns. Another journalist, Armstrong Williams, had been paid $240,000 to champion controversial government programmes through the print, radio and television media.[14]

In early 2002, the British writer and philosopher Roger Scruton was sacked from his position as a *Financial Times* and *Wall Street Journal* columnist after admitting that he had been paid thousands of pounds by the manufacturers of Camel cigarettes to place pro-smoking articles in the UK press.[15]

'We would aim to place an article every two months in one or other of the WSJ (*Wall Street Journal*), *The Times*, the *Telegraph*, the *Spectator*, the *Financial Times*, *The*

Economist, the *Independent* or the *New Statesman*', Scruton had written in a leaked email to his employers.[16]

Japan Tobacco had paid Scruton £4,500 a month for his services, and in return he had written several pieces attacking international plans to impose tighter controls on tobacco firms. In the *Telegraph* in June 2001, Scruton had accused the World Trade Organisation of being controlled by 'anti-smoking fanatics'.[17] The previous year he had produced a paper on the same issue for a libertarian think tank, the Institute of Economic Affairs, in which he condemned the World Health Organisation for a 'lack of honesty and transparency'.[18]

Scruton claimed to have made no secret of his tobacco links, but reportedly neither the *Financial Times* nor the *Wall Street Journal* had been aware of them – and without doing extensive background research, readers of his articles would also have been none the wiser.

As intriguing as the story itself was the reaction from other columnists. Writing in the *Independent*,[19] the writer Terence Blacker noted 'the joy of sanctimonious liberals everywhere' over Scruton's fall from grace:

> The assumption ... appears to be that those who express opinions in the media should be pure in heart and mind, utterly uncontaminated by any outside influence. As anyone who has done this kind of work will know, this is rarely, if ever, likely to be true.
>
> A whole range of pressures ... most of them less

honest and explicit than an annual bung from a tobacco firm, is brought to bear upon the press opinion-monger. He is required to be contrary and interesting ... Rival newspapers should be mentioned rarely and, if possible, unfavourably. Any particular bias, hang-up or enthusiasm of those who commission him must be taken carefully into consideration ...

Only occasionally does this require an out-and-out distortion of what he believes. More often it is a question of what is professionally known as 'compromise': certain, acceptable views should be revealed to the full sunlight while other, less acceptable ones remain in the shadows.

Newcomers ... become aware of the process slowly. They notice that, should they be unwilling to express a particular view, then a rival will quickly be found who will. Soon, the process of corruption becomes ingrained ... Instinctively, the professional columnist will know what is expected.

The campaign for real news

There is no point denying it – I'm a net news addict, and it's getting worse. A few years back I was a fairly light user – BBC, ITN, the occasional broadsheet dalliance on the weekends. But since then it's been spiralling out of all control. I'm now doing everything from the *Qatar Gulf*

Times to the South African *Mail and Guardian*. I've been through broadsheets, dailies, weeklies, journals, gazettes and periodicals. I've done blogs, podcasts, wikis, tickers and RSS feeds, and I've devoured news of every flavour: world, domestic, sports, political, arts, technology, religious, financial, citizen journalist and parish council.

What you start to notice, after a while, is just how many inconsistencies there can be between different news reports covering the same story – not only in the basic details like names, dates and times, but also in the facts that some reporters include and others choose to leave out entirely. We might find our hearts warmed, for example, by the rags-to-riches tale of a kindly international tycoon who is rescuing our local football club from bankruptcy – only to discover from another mainstream source that he has a string of criminal convictions and a track record of lavishing five-star holidays on tabloid journalists, and has recently hired a major PR firm to help him 'tell his side of the story'. Or we may read a piece about a government whistleblower, mentioning in passing his arrest last year on suspicion of fraud – and only discover elsewhere that no charges ever resulted from the arrest, that there was never any evidence against him, and that he's now bringing a civil case for harassment.

Recently I've started getting into all this 'self-referential' news – it's an addict's dream. There's The Media Standards Trust,[20] Fairness and Accuracy in Reporting,[21]

Sourcewatch[22] and the Center for Public Integrity,[23] to name just a few. These people do in-depth reports on how the news gets made – who's funding the lobbyists, think tanks and special interest groups, and the undisclosed affiliations of the supposedly 'independent' experts being put forward by one PR firm or another. Then there are the groups like Reporters Without Borders,[24] Index on Censorship[25] and the Press Gazette,[26] who look at the practical challenges faced by journalists trying to do their job – from the frivolous libel suits by super-sheikhs and oligarchs keen to bury a shady past, to the strong-arm tactics of governments bent on stifling criticism.

In the run-up to the first Gulf War – when the global TV networks were uncritically relaying Hill and Knowlton's 'video news releases', paid for by the Kuwaiti government, into living rooms the world over – most of us would see one or two TV news reports a day, and perhaps look at one newspaper. While there was a small measure of choice in deciding which newspaper to buy and which news programme to watch, what was on offer from each was essentially a 'set menu' of stories, chosen by editors whose job it was to decide on our behalf what was, and was not, 'news'.

Very few of us would have had time to wade through every newspaper produced that day in search of the topics that interested us. And fewer still would have had the resources to do our own background checks on the stories being presented to us as fact. When bias, distortion and outright fabrication crept in, there really wasn't much that we could do about it – most of the people, most of the time, wouldn't even know that it was going on. This at least partly explains the case of 'Nurse Nayirah', among many others.

For decades, the key to bamboozling the general public has been to bamboozle the people who make the news. Over the last century, the PR industry has perfected the art of fooling journalists, knowing that once they'd captured the hearts and minds of the media 'gatekeepers' the battle would be more or less won. By focusing relentlessly on just a few hundred high-profile opinion formers, a PR company could ensure that thousands, if not millions, would receive their message sympathetically.

But the development of the internet has started to shift the balance. In place of the dumbed-down set menu of a broadsheet newspaper circa 1991, we can now get our online information 'à la carte' from a wide range of different sources. Alongside our traditional national media, we can access mainstream news from all over the world. In addition, some other long-established public organisations, such as Amnesty International, Oxfam and the UN, also now publish their own news directly, as do many corporations, universities and national governments. Documents to which journalists alone would traditionally have had exclusive access are often now available online for anyone to look at. If we're sceptical about the way the media has reported on a proposed new law, or summarised a parliamentary or congressional hearing, or covered the latest public statement from Amnesty, Coca Cola or Harvard, we can now go on the internet and read the original text for ourselves.

Having such a wide choice not only means that we can 'pick our own news', but also allows us to build up a fuller picture about an issue that we're interested in, and do background research on the reliability of stories that we find online. By reading a range of accounts from a variety of different sources, rather than just a handful, we can counteract some of the bias within an individual report, and look for evidence of error or distortion.

There is one obvious problem with all of this, of course – how do we gauge the reliability of a random news website that we've just stumbled upon and know almost nothing about? We may find it entertaining to read gobsmacking online claims about the love life of a high-profile celebrity, or shady dealings by a well-known international businessman, but if we have no way of checking whether or not these claims are actually *true*, then they're ultimately not much use to us as news.

Despite all the potential for distortion within the mainstream media, there are still some minimal external checks that help to deter outright fabrication. While the libel laws are often abused by those bent on suppressing legitimate criticism, their existence does give journalists a strong incentive to avoid saying bad things about a living person without good evidence. And while some journalists seem to care more than others about maintaining a reputation for honest and accurate reporting, there are clear professional and commercial benefits to be had in keeping to some basic standards.

But when we're reading information online, we may often not even know which country the website is based in, let alone the motivations, expertise and track record of the author. What looks at first glance like a respectable internet news service – producing thought-provoking articles, with pictures, in an eminently sensible font – may turn out on closer inspection to be a hornet's nest of unsubstantiated rumour, speculation, crank science and conspiracy theory.

Yet there are some things we can do to limit the risk of being duped online. The basic rule of thumb is that we don't accept any information from an untested online source until we've found at least one well-established *mainstream* source that can corroborate it. Some of the more useful amateur news sites work so well not because they contain much original content of their own, but because the author regularly identifies, collates and summarises, with references, a wide range of mainstream new stories about a topic that interests us – be it golf, Uzbekistan or Dulwich FC – thereby saving us the trouble of doing the legwork ourselves.

While it's unwise to trust a claim made on a news blog in isolation, blogs can be a good source of leads to mainstream stories that we might not otherwise have known about. This can cut down the time it takes to find useful information, and should, in principle, leave us no more at risk of being fooled than if we'd got the same details by wading through the paper edition.

One great advantage of the internet is that it helps us to see just how inaccurate – and prone to manipulation – mainstream news reports can sometimes be. The net has also made it far easier to do background checks on the people and organisations being presented as author-ities on some subject or another. If an organisation is endorsed, how long has this organisation existed? How is it funded? Is it using a name very similar to a much more longstanding, well-respected institution? Does it have the same address as a public relations company? Are human sources named or anonymous? If a person is quoted as an 'expert', what are their qualifications and what is their track record? Are they genuinely independent? Do they have any criminal convictions?

CHAPTER FIVE

FAKE EXPERTS AND
NON-DENIAL DENIALS

Between 2002 and 2006, the *Sunday Telegraph* journalist Christopher Booker wrote a series of columns downplaying the dangers of asbestos.[1] Booker's initial claim was that white asbestos had, 'by one of the most unfortunate sleights of hand in scientific history', been unjustly subjected to the same 'demonisation' as the lethal blue and brown varieties, 'just because it shares the same name'. The 'soft, silky fibres' of white asbestos, Booker explained, were 'chemically identical to talcum powder'.[2]

One of Booker's main sources was John Bridle, a man he initially described[3] as 'an experienced South Wales surveyor and qualified chemist'.[4] By 2003, Bridle was 'one of the country's leading asbestos experts'.[5] By 2006 he was Professor John Bridle, a 'knowledgeable and brave whistle-blower'[6] who had helped expose a conspiracy by French and Belgian asbestos-replacement manufacturers,[7] and decontamination companies, to scare the public into removing white asbestos from their homes on the basis of a 'non-existent' risk.[8]

With the support of Booker and his column, Bridle set up the Asbestos Watchdog, 'a company dedicated to giving honest advice to the ever-larger number of people who were victims of the racket'.[9] Bridle, it was claimed, had helped hundreds of *Telegraph* readers in this way, saving millions of pounds.[10] Questions had been raised in Parliament.[11] Bridle's expertise had supposedly been recognised by the Health and Safety Executive, who had taken him on as a 'stakeholder'.[12] White asbestos – henceforth to be known by the mineral name of its main ingredient, 'chrysotile' – posed 'no measurable risk to health'.[13]

But a 2006 investigation by the BBC's *You and Yours* programme accused John Bridle of basing his reputation on 'lies about his credentials, unaccredited tests, and self-aggrandisement'.[14] The investigation highlighted Bridle's 2005 conviction for breaching the Trades Descriptions Act.[15] Bridle had claimed, falsely, to have been awarded a professional asbestos inspection qualification by the British Occupational Hygiene Society (BOHS). In fact he had failed the BOHS test on three separate occasions.

The BBC also examined Bridle's academic credentials. Bridle's website claimed that he had been awarded an honorary degree in 'Asbestos Sciences' from the Russian Academy of Sciences, making him 'the foremost authority on asbestos science in the world',[16] yet when the BBC spoke to them directly, the Academy denied having ever heard of him. Dr Garry Burdett, the principal scientist at the government's Health and Safety Laboratory,[17] expressed surprise that someone who had not published a single scientific research paper should make such a claim.

John Bridle was able to produce a certificate awarding him an 'honorary degree' from an organisation calling itself the Russian Academy of *Medical* Sciences. Yet despite the similarity between the two names, this small organisation had no connection with the prestigious, internationally recognised Russian Academy of Sciences.

Nor was it true – as I discovered when I got in touch with the Health and Safety Executive myself – that Bridle had received any endorsement from the HSE. The 'stakeholder' label was, I was told, a generic civil service term, applicable to anyone who had contacted a government department to declare an interest in an issue that that department was covering – it didn't entail any recognition of Bridle's claimed expertise. Strictly speaking, one could become a 'stakeholder' on the asbestos issue simply by ringing up the Health and Safety Executive, or writing them a letter.[18]

But most striking of all were Bridle's claims about white asbestos, which was banned in the UK in 1999[19] and largely prohibited Europe-wide in 2005.[20] Bridle had visited a number of businesses and private homes where the presence of asbestos was suspected, and offered advice based on what he claimed was expert scientific knowledge. Yet far from posing 'no measurable risk to health', white asbestos is classified by the International Agency for Research on Cancer as a 'group one carcinogen'.[21] Based on a series of peer-reviewed studies,[22] the British government,[23] the European Union, the World Health Organisation[24] and the

World Trade Organisation[25] all believe that white asbestos is unsafe, and dangerous to health. In reality, the distinction between white asbestos and other forms is to some extent academic, as natural deposits of chrysotile are typically contaminated with other deadly minerals from the outset.[26] Even now, asbestos in its various forms is thought to be responsible for nearly 4,000 deaths in the UK each year.[27]

Alongside the government scientists who spelled out that there was 'no safe level' for chrysotile exposure, the BBC interviewed Michael Braidwood, a 59-year-old former factory worker. Braidwood had worked in a white asbestos processing plant for just eight weeks during the 1970s, drilling slates in a dusty warehouse. He'd been told that the material he was dealing with was entirely safe. Now he was dying of mesothelioma, an incurable asbestos-related cancer. 'It just eats away your lung,' he told the programme, noticeably short of breath, 'there's nothing you can do about it.' When asked if he believed that white asbestos was killing him, Michael Braidwood replied that 'it isn't killing me – it *has* killed me'.

During his four-year campaign against 'the great asbestos scam', Christopher Booker penned more than 35 *Sunday Telegraph* articles downplaying the dangers of chrysotile, endorsed John Bridle's expertise on at least thirteen separate occasions,[28] and condemned everyone from the *Sunday Times*[29] to the UK Environment Agency[30] for 'hysteria', 'scaremongering', and being 'babyishly ignorant' about asbestos. But Booker wasn't the only one to be swayed by Bridle's scientific claims. In a debate in Parliament in 2002, John Bercow MP had picked up the refrain about the 'soft, silky' fibres of chrysotile, endorsing John Bridle as a 'qualified chemist', and warning of the dangers of 'bad science'.[31] Bercow sounded sheepish when interviewed by *You and Yours* four years later:

> If you were to ask me ... did I check his precise qualifications, the honest answer is no I didn't. I think that a lot of people would accept that in life, generally, you tend to take people at face value unless you have a particular reason to suspect them, and I didn't.

Bercow was shocked to learn of Bridle's public statement, on his website that the Conservative Party shadow cabinet was one of his 'clients', and described the claim as 'wrong, far-fetched and misleading'.[32]

Not so Christopher Booker. Writing in his book, *Scared to Death*, in 2007,[33] the veteran columnist condemned the BBC's exposé of John Bridle as a 'farrago of make-believe', based on 'hearsay evidence ... given by Bridle's enemies', 'a carefully planned operation to discredit him', and 'one of the most bizarrely partisan programmes the BBC can ever have broadcast'. The BBC, Booker maintained, 'had allowed itself to be used as a mouthpiece by the very interests which were defrauding the public to the tune of hundreds of millions of pounds a year'.[34] Bridle, he claimed, had considered suing the BBC for libel, but decided this would be too much of a 'gamble', due to the BBC's 'bottomless purse of licence-payers' money'.[35] Instead, he had lodged a complaint with the broadcasting regulator Ofcom. According to Booker, this complaint remained unresolved, due to the BBC continuing to 'spin out the resulting exchanges'.

In the same chapter, Booker accused UK government health officials of 'working hand in glove with [decontamination] contractors to uphold their fraudulent claims',[36] and repeated his assertion that white asbestos cement, being 'essentially harmless', posed 'no measurable risk to health'.[37]

Dusting the fingerprints of the PR industry

A Google search on John Bridle's name turns up several gems, but the warmest praise appears in a 2006 press release from the industry-funded 'Chrysotile Institute' – the modern successor to the 'Asbestos Institute', which was set up with funding from the industry in 1984 (see p. 42).[38] The press release supports Bridle's claim to be 'the foremost authority on asbestos science in the world', and trails a presentation in Bangkok, in which he will

> highlight cases in the United Kingdom where a combination of 'bad science, bad regulation and a campaign of demonisation' has resulted in bank-

ruptcies and a climate of fear about products and materials that present 'no measurable risk to health'.[39]

One vital tool in any political campaign is the 'key message'. This is a punchy form of words that succinctly expresses the main point that you are trying to get across. The secret is then to ensure that this message is repeated as widely and as often as possible. As President George W. Bush once famously told a stunned high school audience: 'In my line of work you got to keep repeating things over and over and over again for the truth to sink in, to kind of catapult the propaganda.'[40]

But while catapulting the propaganda might have served the public relations industry well in recent decades, the internet now poses a problem. Another vital tool of any PR operation is secrecy: with or without catapults, the public is not supposed to know that they are being propagandised. Yet it's now quite easy to 'dust for fingerprints' when we suspect a PR hustle, simply by googling what we think may be the key message and seeing what comes up. At the time of writing, the phrase 'no measurable risk to health' appeared in 40 news sources and blog postings worldwide. All but five were about asbestos – and nearly half were either from John Bridle's Asbestos Watchdog or the Chrysotile Institute. The only mainstream news articles supporting the view that white asbestos posed 'no measurable risk to health' were those by Christopher Booker in the *Sunday Telegraph*.

As a campaign message, 'no measurable risk to health' is a clever choice. By its very nature, the precise risk from any type of asbestos is hard to measure. As with cigarette smoke, only a minority of those exposed will die as a result, and only after several decades. Yet while a smoker may at least have a rough idea of how many cigarettes he or she has smoked, and for how long, a victim of asbestos-related cancer will usually have no way of measuring how much asbestos they inhaled. A further complication is that while natural deposits of white asbestos may *mostly* consist of chrysotile, they usually contain other, even deadlier, minerals, such as tremolite.[41] While animal studies have shown that chrysotile causes cancer even in its pure form, few human victims will have been exposed to it without simultaneously breathing in other forms of asbestos. So at the moment we just don't have much data to go on.

A lawyer might defend the Chrysotile Institute's assertion that their product poses 'no *measurable* risk to health' by pointing out that, strictly speaking, all they meant was that there is (or may be) a risk, but that no precise measurement of that risk is possible. Yet on a cursory reading, one could easily take the Institute's claim to mean that their product poses no *significant* risk, and is essentially safe. Their key message seems to play cleverly on the subtle distinction between an unknown danger and an insignificant one.

In politics, this kind of tactic is sometimes called a 'non-denial denial'. Examples include President Clinton's 'I did not have sexual relations with that woman'[42] when probed about his intern, Monica Lewinsky, and Prime Minister John Major's 'no plans ... to increase VAT [Value Added Tax]', shortly before the 1992 general election.[43] Major's government famously went on to increase VAT within months – pointing out that they hadn't said that they *weren't* going to increase taxes, merely that at that particular moment they had no plans to do so.[44] Clinton and Lewinsky, even more famously, had done a whole lot more than hold hands – yet the President insisted he had told the truth, because *he* was using the term 'sexual relations' in its narrowest possible sense.

A common form of 'non-denial denial' in discussions about science involves claims about evidence. During the late 1980s, UK government ministers repeatedly insisted that there was 'no scientific evidence' that Bovine Spongiform Encephalopathy (BSE), commonly known as 'mad cow disease', could be transmitted to humans. They were right, but what was less well publicised was that the government – allegedly under pressure from the farming industry – had curtailed the very research that could have shown a link.[45] When detailed studies were eventually done, scientists concluded that BSE could be transferred to human beings, and was responsible for at least some cases of the terminal brain disorder Creutzfeldt-Jakob Disease.

There can only be scientific evidence of a health risk once someone has carried out some research – and this takes time and money. Even where a risk has been proven conclusively, there has often been a long delay between the first suspicions and the establishment of comprehensive proof – and a longer delay still before that proof has gained full public acceptance. Generally speaking, the deadlier a health hazard, the easier it will be to come up with evidence about it, simply because there will be more individual cases to examine. But where there is a long delay between cause and effect, as with exposure to cigarette smoke or asbestos, this evidence may take decades to accumulate. And where there is a multi-million-dollar industry whose commercial interests are at stake, the scientific debate will likely be transformed into a full-scale political battle.

The case of John Bridle highlights the difficulty – even for people whose job it is to question and scrutinise – of distinguishing genuine scientific argument from charlatanism. In the absence of expert knowledge of our own, it is easy to allow our political leanings to determine whom we take seriously and whom we ignore. Just as leftist conspiracy theorists often play to fears about the power of government and big business, debunkers such as John Bridle tend to exploit the concerns of the political right. Bridle cleverly tailored his message to appeal to conservative fears about the costs of zealous EU bureaucracy, 'bad science', and disreputable foreign firms fanning public hysteria for their own commercial gain.

Bridle's error was in overstating his case and telling a number of demonstrable lies, which made him easy to discredit, and led to his eventual prosecution under the Trades Descriptions Act in 2005. Given these mistakes, the fact that he was able to influence so many people over such a long period of time is especially striking. Even after Bridle's conviction and public exposure, Christopher Booker has continued to champion his cause and, in the face of repeated public rebuttals, to list asbestos among a number of environmental 'scares' which he believes have been maliciously overstated.[46]

CHAPTER SIX

THE BAREFOOT SCIENTIST AND THE GREAT LEAP FORWARD

When pseudoscience takes hold of a government, the results can be truly catastrophic – and no story illustrates this better than the tale of Trofim Denisovitch Lysenko. The agronomist son of a Ukrainian peasant farmer, Lysenko first rose to prominence in 1927, when the Soviet newspaper *Pravda* credited him with 'turning the barren fields of the Transcaucasus green ... so that cattle will not perish from poor feeding, and the peasant Turk will live through the winter without trembling for tomorrow.'[1] *Pravda* characterised Lysenko as the model of the strong, sullen peasant genius, a 'barefoot scientist' whose practical wisdom was transforming Soviet agriculture. The fact that Lysenko's revolutionary winter pea crops failed the following year, and in all subsequent years, went unreported.

Over the next two decades, Lysenko proved himself adept at self-promotion, charming journalists and party officials alike with his ideologically agreeable theories[2] and grandiose claims about their effectiveness. Just as the proletariat could be moulded into adherence to the principles of communism, Lysenko claimed, so wheat could

71

be trained to thrive in a cold climate by being soaked in freezing water.[3] Lysenko denounced as 'bourgeois' the Darwinian view that organisms of the same species compete against each other for resources. He claimed to have proved that planting wheat seedlings very close together would actually increase productivity.[4]

The barefoot scientist spurned conventional tests in favour of written questionnaires, which farm workers would fill in themselves. Naturally, the figures were usually favourable. 'If you want to obtain a certain result, you will obtain it',[5] Lysenko declared, in terms reminiscent of today's self-help gurus.

At a time when large areas of the USSR faced crippling famine, Lysenko's claims, and the low cost of his methods, proved very attractive to the authorities. *Pravda* continued to follow his progress, hailing each new claimed success as a triumph of Soviet technology. Fellow scientists were less impressed. In 1935, an investigation by a student of the geneticist Nikolai Vavilov found that Lysenko's methods had no statistical effect.[6] Lysenko dismissed the results, and began to attack the use of statistics in science, claiming that mathematics had no relevance to biology.[7] He denounced geneticists as 'fly-lovers and people haters',[8] who preferred to engage in abstract research than address the practical problems of the Soviet worker.

In a speech before Joseph Stalin in 1935, the peasant genius declared, to loud applause from the Soviet leader, that 'a class enemy is always an enemy whether he is a scientist or not'.[9] Lysenko condemned the entire canon of genetics as 'fascist' science, flatly denying the existence of genes,[10] and accusing geneticists of conspiring to destroy the Soviet Union.

In 1938, Lysenko was appointed director of the Soviet Academy of Sciences, a position he used to his full advantage. Dozens of less prominent scientists had already been executed or dismissed when Lysenko's arch-rival, the geneticist Nikolai Vavilov, was arrested in 1940 as a defender of 'bourgeois pseudoscience'. Vavilov died in prison, of malnutrition, three years later.

Lysenko's influence began to decline following the death of Stalin in 1953, but many of his ideas were still current in 1958, when Mao Zedong, an avid admirer of Soviet science, began planning his 'Great Leap Forward'.

Of all the man-made catastrophes in history, the Chinese famine that claimed 30 million lives between 1958 and 1961 must be among the worst.[11] Chief responsibility rests with Chairman Mao and his followers, who had forced through a series of disastrous agricultural reforms. But if Mao was the main architect of the disaster, Trofim Lysenko, whose theories he aggressively promoted, surely deserves the title of junior draughtsman.

The collectivisation of farming, which Mao had been pushing since the early 1950s, was dramatically accelerated. Farmers were instructed to adopt Lysenko's method of 'close planting', and stop all use of chemical fertilisers.[12] In keeping with the theories of Lysenko's colleague Teventy

Maltsev,[13] farm labourers were made to plant their seeds much deeper than usual, at a depth of three to four feet. A third of all land was to be left fallow.

These measures, combined with a highly effective Maoist campaign to kill every sparrow in China, had a catastrophic effect.[14] Food production plummeted, and although the extermination of the sparrows meant less grain was eaten by birds, the insect population exploded. 1959 saw China's worst locust infestation in history. The little surplus food that had survived Lysenko's agricultural quackery was devoured in a plague of biblical proportions.

Cannibalism became widespread. Eyewitness accounts tell of people eating cats, dogs and insects, and of parents feeding dying children on their own blood. Matters were made worse by the communist regime's systemic denial of what was going on. Officials carried on reporting bumper harvests, refused all offers of foreign assistance, and doubled exports of grain.[15] Doctors were instructed to record 'natural causes' on the death certificates of famine victims. When another senior communist official, Peng Dehuai, tried to alert Mao to the problems the country was facing, he was labelled a 'rightist' and purged.[16]

There is some evidence that Mao himself was genuinely unaware of the extent of the disasters he had wrought on his countrymen. By constructing a state apparatus that so strongly deterred the reporting of anything but good news, Mao made it impossible for anyone, even those at the top, to see the true picture.

Mao's delusions were not confined to his own circle. A succession of foreign observers, from the BBC's Felix Greene[17] to the future French president, François Mitterand, were taken on tours of China, and declared that all was well. Mitterand uncritically repeated Mao's assertion that 'the people of China have never been near famine'.[18] Yet by 1961, the problems were becoming impossible to ignore. Fearing civil unrest, moderates within the party forced Mao to abandon the Great Leap Forward and reverse his failed agricultural reforms. By the time food production had returned to normal, tens of millions were dead – though it would be another two decades before the full scale of the catastrophe was acknowledged.

Trofim Lysenko's demise began in 1962 with his denunciation by three prominent Soviet physicists: Yakov Borisovich Zel'dovich, Vitaly Ginzburg and Pyotr Kapitsa. Two years later, the renowned physicist Andrei Sakharov roundly condemned Lysenko, in a speech to the General Assembly of the Soviet Academy of Sciences:

> He is responsible for the shameful backwardness of Soviet biology and of genetics in particular, for the dissemination of pseudo-scientific views, for adventurism, for the degradation of learning, and for the defamation, firing, arrest, even death, of many genuine scientists.[19]

The Soviet press, once enamoured of Trofim Lysenko,

now turned on him, and he was quickly removed from his academic post. Later that year, an expert commission was appointed to investigate his work. The results were damning, and Lysenko's reputation was destroyed. Nikolai Vavilov, and the other geneticists who had been persecuted at Lysenko's behest, were rehabilitated. Stalin's 'barefoot scientist' died in relative obscurity in 1976.

Trofim Lysenko held sway over Soviet science for three decades before he was fully exposed. He survived for so long by ruthlessly manipulating the political climate to protect his work from scientific scrutiny. In a totalitarian society, as so many of Lysenko's critics discovered, the price of scepticism can be fatal. It was no coincidence that Lysenko's downfall came at the hands of nuclear physicists. This was the one group of Soviet scientists who, due to the political importance of their work, were relatively well protected and thus much freer to speak out than their peers. One lesson must be that unless a society allows room for scepticism – unless scepticism is built into the institutions of the state – it can leave itself vulnerable to fraud and corruption, with catastrophic results.

One characteristic feature of pseudoscience is the use of vague and unreliable methods. We can see this most clearly in Lysenko's reluctance to use conventional measures of crop productivity, preferring instead to get farm workers to fill in questionnaires which could not be independently verified.

As with most pseudoscientists, Lysenko's arguments

were primarily aimed at public opinion and the political elite, rather than the scientific community. It was for this reason that he routinely used political rhetoric, rather than scientific arguments, to dismiss competing theories. Lysenko condemned Darwinist biology as 'bourgeois' and 'fascist'. Geneticists were 'fly-lovers and people haters'. His scientific opponents were 'class enemies'.[20]

But where Lysenko truly excelled was in deliberately evading scrutiny by other scientists. His method for achieving this was simple yet effective: anyone who disagreed with him was liable to get killed. The word 'Lysenkoism' is today synonymous with dubious scientific theories that gain credence through strong-arm tactics and political patronage.

CHAPTER SEVEN

DON'T GET FOOLED
BY BOGUS SCEPTICS

There is a meaningful difference between being a sceptic and being in denial. Sceptics form their beliefs on the basis of concrete facts, and evaluate each piece of evidence on its own merits. Denialists select their facts on the basis of their pre-existing beliefs, and reject evidence that they dislike, or find inconvenient.[1]

When faced with two competing theories, the denialist chooses the one that best fits his or her political, emotional, religious or commercial predilections, and then declares themselves 'sceptical' about the alternative, however over-whelming the evidence in its favour. So alongside the 'sceptics' about the link between smoking and cancer,[2] there are the self-described '911 sceptics' who claim that the World Trade Centre attack was an inside job,[3] the so-called 'Aids sceptics' who deny that HIV exists,[4] and the 'Holocaust sceptics' who deny that millions of Jews were murdered by the Nazis.[5]

Most notorious among these is the discredited historian David Irving.[6] Irving began writing in the 1960s, and managed to gain public acceptance as an academic – albeit a controversial one – with a series of books on the Nazi regime. But during the late 1980s he began to go further. Irving claimed to be sceptical about the documentary and eyewitness evidence for the Holocaust, and argued that forensic tests carried out on the walls of the Auschwitz gas chambers proved that they had not been used for mass executions.[7]

Irving's assertions drew widespread criticism from other historians, including the US academic Deborah Lipstadt. In her 1993 book *Denying the Holocaust*, Lipstadt labelled Irving a 'holocaust denier' and 'falsifier of history'.[8] In response, Irving launched a libel action – but the move backfired catastrophically. Following a lengthy trial, in which Irving's work was examined in fine detail by expert witnesses, a UK judge, Justice Gray, rejected his complaint. Gray concluded in April 2000 that:

> Irving has for his own ideological reasons persistently and deliberately misrepresented and manipulated historical evidence; that for the same reasons he has portrayed Hitler in an unwarrantedly favourable light, principally in relation to his attitude towards and responsibility for the treatment of the Jews; that he is an active Holocaust denier; that he is anti-semitic and racist and that he associates with right-wing extremists who promote neo-Nazism.[9]

Lipstadt's court victory was all the more damning because, under English law, the burden of proof had rested with her – it was she, not Irving, who was required to prove beyond reasonable doubt that she was telling the truth.

The historian Richard Evans, acting as an expert witness for the defence, had painstakingly checked hundreds of the historical sources that Irving had cited as evidence in support of his theories over his 30-year career. He concluded that Irving had 'fallen so far short of the standards of scholarship customary among historians that he doesn't deserve to be called a historian at all.'[10] Evans declared himself shocked 'at the sheer depths of duplicity' he found. For three decades David Irving had systematically misrepresented the documents that he claimed supported his view. Irving's work was rejected even by the historians he had subpoenaed to support him, with one, Sir John Keegan, arguing that Irving's claim that Hitler was unaware of the Holocaust 'defies common sense'.[11]

The characteristic feature of 'false scepticism' is that it centres not on an impartial search for the truth, but on the defence of a preconceived ideological position or vested interest. David Irving's denial of the established facts of the Holocaust was motivated not by a sceptical open-mindedness, but rather the opposite – his prior sympathies had driven him to falsify history, so as to paint Hitler and the Nazis in a more sympathetic light.

One giveaway sign is a habit common within all forms of pseudo-scholarship – a double standard in the evaluation of evidence. The tobacco industry 'sceptic' Clarence Cook Little downplayed the value of animal experimentation when the results supported the smoking–cancer link, but enthusiastically endorsed such studies when they seemed to show that smoking was safe.[12] Likewise, David Irving was rigorously sceptical about the eyewitness testimonies of Holocaust survivors, but uncritically accepted Nazi claims about the number of financial crimes committed by German Jews during the 1930s.

Another tell-tale sign is the refusal to specify what would count as acceptable evidence.[13] Genuine sceptics are at least prepared to define what it would take to convince them. Many of us, for example, are sceptical about the claim that super-intelligent aliens are regularly visiting the Earth for unspecified reasons. But we can also quite easily conceive of circumstances under which we might reconsider that view – for example if a squadron of UFOs landed in Hyde Park and a cohort of little green men marched on Westminster.

Had Irving applied the same level of scepticism to all historical facts as he did to the facts about the Holocaust, then it would have been difficult to maintain a belief in the reality of any event that he had not personally witnessed. In the words of the historians David Oshinsky and Michael Curtis: 'If the Holocaust is not a fact, then nothing is a fact.'[14] Our knowledge about the French Revolution, the rise and fall of the Roman Empire and the life and times of Napoleon Bonaparte all rest on evidence which could, in some theoretically possible alternative reality, have been faked, exaggerated, misread or distorted through some vast international conspiracy. Eyewitnesses can lie or be mistaken, documents can be forged and archaeological evidence can be radically misinterpreted. All accounts of history are imperfect, incomplete and potentially subject to revision.

To say that all human evidence is fallible is to make a valid point about the limits of knowledge, and the nature of 'certainty'. But to use this argument selectively – to use it as a basis for debunking and rejecting only those established facts to which one takes personal exception, while setting a much lower evidential standard for claims that one finds agreeable – is quite the opposite of genuine scepticism.

Atrocity denial – or 'negationism' – often also has a clear political motivation, and Irving is by no means unique. Those with ideological sympathies towards communism have likewise sought to downplay the true extent of the atrocities of Joseph Stalin and Mao Zedong. Many Turks still deny that the Armenian genocide ever took place, and insist that the accusation arises from a sinister international conspiracy against their country.[15] In Central Africa, many with a vested interest still deny that genocide took place in Rwanda in 1994,[16] notwithstanding the piles of skulls and detailed eyewitness testimonies.

'Scepticism' about scientific evidence of risks to our health or to the environment, meanwhile, more often has a commercial vested interest at its heart. The model developed by the tobacco industry in the 1950s has become a template for any industry that finds itself troubled by evidence that its products are harmful, from asbestos to the global warming 'controversy'.[17] More sweeping denials about science are often based on an attempt to defend the authority of a particular religious perspective. It's difficult, for example, to find 'sceptics' about Darwin's theory of evolution except among those who have a strong commitment to the literal truth of the Christian Bible.

But the flip side of denialism is that it often involves the uncritical acceptance of a flimsy and convoluted 'alternative' explanation. In rejecting one of the strongest theories in modern biology in favour of a pseudoscience based on the literal interpretation of the Bible, 'Darwin sceptics' have been left trying to explain the existence of kangaroos in Australia by suggesting that they may have hopped off Noah's Ark and 'rafted on mats of vegetation' to Oz as the waters receded after the Great Flood.[18] Holocaust deniers, likewise, declare themselves 'sceptical' about eyewitness accounts of Nazi atrocities by concentration camp survivors, yet show no such scepticism towards those who allege, without evidence, that thousands of historians around the world have been engaged in a 60-year global conspiracy to smear Adolf Hitler.[19] And '9/11 sceptics', such as the former MI5 agent David Shayler,[20] reject the hypothesis that the Twin Towers collapse was caused by two fuel-laden passenger jets flying into the buildings in quick succession, but seem to have no trouble believing that the plane crashes, witnessed by thousands of New Yorkers, were nothing but a cleverly-constructed holographic projection.[21]

CHAPTER EIGHT

CHAOS, CONSPIRACY
AND THE BLAME GAME

Paranoia can have deadly consequences. In Rwanda, in 1994, genocide was triggered by rumours of a secret plot by Tutsis to seize power and restore their ethnic group's domination of the Hutu majority.[1] During the Middle Ages, hundreds of men and women were burned at the stake as witches, supposedly in league with the devil. Later in this book we will see how the conspiracy theories surrounding HIV and Aids may have cost thousands of lives in Africa.

Yet while an imagined conspiracy can do enormous damage, there have been plenty of cases where a seemingly outlandish tale turned out to be true. From the 1985 New Zealand bomb attack on the Greenpeace ship *Rainbow Warrior* by the French intelligence services[2] and the complicity of UK forces in paramilitary killings in Northern Ireland[3] to the Enron scandal[4] and the Catholic Church's cover-up of abuse by paedophile priests,[5] there are numerous examples of disreputable behaviour by seemingly respectable organisations.

Then there are the stories that are just plain odd. A few years ago, while volunteering for a human rights group in south-east Asia, I received a series of emails claiming that a group of ethnic Hmong tribesmen, who had fought on the side of the Americans in the Indo-China war, were still holed up with their families in the jungles of Laos, constantly on the run from the Lao and Vietnamese armies. The emails directed us to an amateurish website with lurid colours, typos galore and the names and photographs of the people it called the 'secret war veterans', along with dates of their alleged skirmishes with the military forces intent on wiping them out.[6]

We ignored the issue, figuring that the media would have cottoned on long ago if it was anything more than a conspiracy theory. But then, several weeks later, *Time* magazine ran a front-page exposé, backing up the bulk of our email correspondent's claims.[7] A journalist and photographer had travelled into the Lao jungle and found the Hmong survivors. *Time* carried a long report with pages of photographs, and a detailed account of how the group had survived for the past 27 years. While there were still many unanswered questions, the Lao government could no longer deny that they existed.

One thing that was strikingly different about this case, when I compared it with most other conspiracy rumours I had heard, was that the claims had been very clear and detailed. The main focus of the story was the existence of a specific group of people in a specific location, with names, dates and pictures – and these were details that could, in principle, be checked. By contrast, many conspiracy claims focus on things that are very vague or difficult to verify – a secret, unwritten deal between businessmen and world leaders, an obscure technical reinterpretation of a long-established scientific theory, or an earth-shattering secret locked away in a military facility that is, by necessity, inaccessible to the public.

Neither did the story about the Hmong 'secret war veterans' require us to turn our understanding of the world upside down, as many of the more outlandish conspiracy theories do. The CIA's participation was marginal. Alien lizards were not involved, and neither was Elvis or the British royal family. And while it was a surprise to learn that Laos' communist government had been able to cover up the issue for so long, the regime's closed and secretive nature had been well documented. It was far easier to see how the case could have been kept from public scrutiny in a country like Laos than in a freer and more open society.

Something that did change, however, was my understanding of the media. The story of the Hmong 'secret war veterans' seems to show that in remote corners of authoritarian countries, all sorts of things can go on without the international press having any inkling. Just as you shouldn't believe everything you read in the papers, neither should you assume, a priori, that everything that isn't in the papers isn't true.

The term 'conspiracy theory' is itself a contentious one.

Strictly speaking, any theory that asserts the existence of a conspiracy – such as, for example, the claim that Guy Fawkes plotted to blow up the English parliament in 1605 – could be described as a conspiracy theory. But the term is nonetheless a useful shorthand for theories which cry 'conspiracy!' on the basis of highly questionable – or non-existent – evidence. Whereas Guy Fawkes was found hiding in the cellars of the House of Lords, in possession of several large barrels of gunpowder, with a rudimentary fuse and several matches in his pocket,[8] there is a notable lack of proof that would convict the entire medical establishment of jointly conspiring, as some claim, to commit 'pharmacological genocide'.[9] It's this lack of proof that makes the latter assertion a 'conspiracy theory' in the commonly understood sense of the term.

Conspiracy theories are fun. It's much more interesting to suppose that Princess Diana died as a result of a shady plot involving MI6 and the Duke of Edinburgh than through a random, purposeless combination of drink, drugs and bad driving. It's far more exciting to believe that HIV–Aids is the 'mythical' product of a vast, twenty-year, billion-dollar conspiracy[10] (and a racist one at that) to demonise Africans and protect the profits of the dastardly drug companies than that the disease is just another nasty fatal illness. The world of 'false flags', fake moon landings, aliens and 'Illuminati' is an exhilarating place to be.

Conspiracy theories often appeal to our love of a good story. But they can also pander to popular prejudices and fears – from the anti-Semitic conspiracy myths embraced by the Nazis to the 'kill or be killed' rumours that helped to trigger the 1994 Rwandan genocide. And although the details of the alleged plots are often implausibly intricate and complex, the overall picture of events being ruthlessly controlled by a small elite group is seductively simple. Such explanations hold out the hope that if only this devilish elite could be exposed and defeated, the global problems for which we blame them could also be eradicated.

Extreme conspiracy theories often credit those in charge of the alleged plot with extraordinary power to control events and prevent unforeseen mishaps. Critics of 9/11 conspiracy theories point out that, in order to maintain the deception, the US government would have to have enlisted the co-operation of thousands of willing agents, and persuaded them all to remain silent about the conspiracy. Just one insider-turned-whistleblower could have exposed the entire scheme – and yet this has never happened.[11] The '9/11 sceptics' may be paranoid, but they also demonstrate a striking faith in the ability of human beings to impose their will – albeit with evil intentions – on a chaotic universe.[12]

Another thing that we see very clearly with the 9/11 conspiracy theories is a tendency to treat tenuous reinterpretations of the accepted evidence as if they constitute a knock-down refutation. Much has been made of video footage of the collapse of the World Trade Centre, where clouds of dust or smoke can be seen billowing from each floor in sequence as the towers implode. According to demolition experts, the video simply shows dust and smoke being squeezed out in a concertina effect as each floor buckles and collapses into the one below it.[13] But some conspiracy theorists insist that the footage shows that the buildings were brought down by a series of controlled explosions.

And while proponents of conspiracy theories often present themselves as open-minded sceptics, seeking merely to establish the truth behind the 'official story', their accounts can often become dogmatic. Rachel North,[14] one of the survivors of the 7 July 2005 London bombings, has sought to confront the conspiracy theorists who claim that the explosions were caused by a 'power surge', rather than by bombs, and that this was then covered up by the authorities. North argues that survivors like herself are best placed to know what they saw, and that a power surge could never have caused the horrific injuries she witnessed. In response, the conspiracy theorist David Shayler has suggested that Rachel North is not a genuine survivor, but an agent – or possibly a 'composite' of several agents – working for the British security services.[15]

This tendency to dismiss counter-evidence by postulating an even larger conspiracy is a characteristic feature of many global conspiracy theories. The end result can be a complex and convoluted, yet internally consistent, account of the world, in which the lack of concrete evidence is simply taken as further proof of the extraordinary power of the conspirators to cover up their activities.

The most extreme conspiracy theories are thus constructed in a way that makes them impossible to check or verify. If someone believes with absolute certainty that everything they see and hear is being corrupted and distorted by an all-powerful invisible elite, then there is no proof we could ever offer them that would count as a refutation. Conflicting evidence can always be explained away as a fabrication. Dissenting voices can be dismissed as paid agents or duped patsies. In order to disprove such a theory, we would need to disprove the existence of something that is, by definition, impossible to detect. And, as the philosopher Descartes found when he tried to disprove his own speculations about the existence of an invisible demon secretly controlling his senses, this is a nigh-on impossible task.[16]

The story of David Shayler offers a striking insight into the mindset of the most extreme conspiracy theorists. A former British agent, Shayler rose to prominence in the late 1990s with a series of revelations about the activities of MI5 and MI6, for which he was subsequently prosecuted under the Official Secrets Act. Following the terrorist attacks on the World Trade Centre in September 2001, Shayler became a UK spokesman for the collection of groups who claim that '9/11 was an inside job', championing the view that what appeared to be planes were in fact holographic projections. He pursued a similar line following the London bombings, culminating in his wild accusations about the survivor Rachel North.

Then, in July 2007, Shayler stunned Glastonbury Town Hall[17] with the announcement that he was the reincarnation of Jesus Christ. He followed this up with a media release[18] confirming that 'I am God incarnated as spirit and man', and called a press conference in which he was to give further details: 'Journalists are asked to arrive with an open mind as this is a truth which they are in no position to determine and they may be risking their chances of eternal life.'

The reaction among Shayler's fellow 'sceptics' was swift and seemingly effortless: 'Mr Shayler has been very well groomed and cross-media marketed for the last couple of years and the reason has now been revealed', wrote one blogger.[19] In the topsy-turvy world of committed conspiracism, almost any development can be dissolved and reconstituted as further proof of the power of the wicked elite. David Shayler had, the conspiracists concluded, been sent by MI5 to infiltrate the '7/7 truth movement', rise to the top, and then discredit them all with crazy talk about being the son of God.

The difference between conspiracy fact and conspiracy theory comes down, ultimately, to evidence – photographs and forensics, letters and memos, film and audio recordings, witness statements and public confessions. The more detailed that evidence, and the more diverse the sources that back it up, the more difficult it will have been to fake. One tell-tale sign that you may be dealing with a hoaxer or a fantasist is when you're being told that, for one reason or another, the evidence can't be accessed or revealed.

But it's not only foil-hat-wearing loners who can be seduced by conspiracism, even in a well-established democracy. Arguably the most influential conspiracy theory of the early 21st century was the claim by the British and US governments in 2002 and 2003 that Iraq was secretly developing 'weapons of mass destruction'.

Where the '9/11 Truthers' had the film *Loose Change*, which expertly wove a web of half-truths into a seemingly compelling case for the World Trade Centre having been brought down by a controlled explosion, the 'WMD Truthers' had the infamous British government 'dossiers',[20] which cobbled together a potent mix of hearsay, rumour and distortion[21] in an effort to convince the world that Iraq had chemical, biological or nuclear weapons. To add further weight to this claim, Britain's prime minister, Tony Blair, declared that he himself had been shown even more convincing evidence about Iraq's WMD, but that for security reasons he was, regrettably, unable to reveal it. The argument was made all the more urgent by the claim that these weapons could be battle-ready – and capable of striking at a British target – with just 45 minutes' notice.[22]

Some were convinced, but others remained sceptical.

Suspicions were aroused by the fact that the British and US governments seemed intent on stopping the work of the UN inspectors who were in Iraq trying to determine whether the regime had any banned weapons. Striking, too, was the extent to which advocates of war chose to interpret the lack of evidence for WMD not as a reason for thinking that the weapons might not exist, but rather as further proof of the Iraqi regime's devious and untrustworthy nature. As each new inspection drew a blank, rumours were spread that the weapons might have been hidden in Syria,[23] or buried in the desert. Some within the US government sought to characterise the inspectors as incompetent or ineffectual – thus undermining the sole available source of independent verification.

There were, of course, no weapons of mass destruction and no conspiracy to acquire them. The public had, famously, been sold another pig in a poke. The intelligence that Tony Blair had been shown in secret was no less 'dodgy' than what had been made public – and the result was Britain's most disastrous military adventure since Suez. Even after Iraq had been invaded by British and American forces, and no banned weapons found, US defence secretary Donald Rumsfeld continued to insist that 'absence of evidence is not evidence of absence'[24] – a phrase much beloved, ironically, of those who believe that governments around the world are covering up the existence of UFOs.[25]

'It's very frustrating, as a minor participant, to have

learned afterwards that that the head of MI6 felt the intelligence was being made to fit around the policy', John Williams, one of the government press officers involved in drawing up the 'dodgy dossiers', later wrote. 'I took the intelligence seriously. Nobody ever cast doubt on it in my presence at the time.' In hindsight, Williams concluded, 'we could have done with a heavy dose of scepticism'.[26]

Some people take John Williams' account at face value. Others have found it impossible to believe that neither he nor his colleagues thought to question the intelligence, when so many in the wider public were so openly incredulous. But perhaps the more terrifying thought is that Williams might have been telling the truth – that despite the transparently flimsy nature of the supposed evidence, the British and US governments really had convinced themselves that the claims about WMD were true. The next chapter will look at the phenomenon known as 'groupthink'.

CHAPTER NINE

GROUPTHINK

My default brain position aboard 'Earth Orbiter One'
was that we were 200 kilometres up, travelling at
about seven kilometres per second. Too many things
were telling me that for me to think otherwise. The
simulator was too damned convincing. The Earth
looked too serenely real whenever the pilots ushered
us forward to the cockpit to view it.

Charlie Skelton, actor[1]

In December 2005, Channel 4 aired a reality TV show called *Space Cadets*, in which a group of three volunteers were duped into thinking that they had been sent into orbit around the Earth in a Russian space shuttle. The volunteers had been selected from a larger group, through a series of entertaining TV challenges designed to identify those most prone to psychological 'suggestibility'.[2]

Channel 4 had gone to great lengths to convince the would-be cosmonauts that what they were experiencing was real. The group was assembled at the Biggin Hill airfield, and then flown to what they were told was a Russian military facility in Kazakhstan. In reality, they had been taken on a convoluted four-hour flight around the British Isles before landing at a disused airbase in Suffolk. There, a team of actors, playing the roles of Russian scientists and military personnel, prepared them for their 'mission'. An entire aircraft hangar was set up to look like a launch centre, and a sophisticated space simulator borrowed from a Hollywood film studio was adapted to act as the '*Earth Orbiter One*' shuttle.[3]

The experiment had been carefully constructed, with the help of psychologists, to create a phenomenon known as 'groupthink'. The volunteers had been removed from their normal environment, and immersed in an illusion in which figures of authority – actors playing white-coated scientists and gruff military officers – had an important role. In the process, a powerful social bond had developed between the members of the group; participants had a strong sense that they were all on the same journey, working towards a common goal, and this helped to maintain conformity.

The show reached its climax when the three duped contestants who had been selected to complete the 'mission' were put inside the shuttle simulator – along with three actors who were in on the scam – and made to believe that they were being launched into space. The charade was maintained for five days before the truth was revealed, with the three contestants seemingly convinced throughout, even when obvious 'giveaway' clues were dropped into the mix by the programme's producers. But what was even more remarkable was that when the experiment was over, one of the actors involved, Charlie Skelton, reported having found the illusion so compelling that he was wholly swept up in it, even though he knew, rationally, that it was all a hoax.

'My poor brain is a scramble of half-truths, astronomical lies and unbridled lunacy', he wrote soon after emerging from the experiment. 'I've just scribbled a list of what I know for sure: I've been a mole on a fake reality show called *Space Cadets*; I have a Russian doll in my hand luggage; I've just spent the past five days in a flight simulator in a hangar on the Suffolk coast; and – last but by no means least – I've just spent the past five days in space.'[4]

Skelton's experience – if authentic[5] – highlights how easy it can be to be sucked in by a dominant idea that you know to be false, if for some reason you are prevented from standing up and challenging it. In Skelton's case, he was unable to speak out because his job was to help maintain the deception of the three voluntary participants. In other circumstances, we may be deterred from speaking out through a fear of seeming foolish, disloyal or 'negative'.

One example of groupthink with tragic consequences involved a genuine space mission, the launch of the shuttle *Challenger* in 1986.[6] The day before take-off, engineers working on the shuttle had warned of structural flaws in the booster rockets, and recommended calling off the launch. But NASA decision-makers, anxious to avoid a politically embarrassing delay, refused to accept this and persuaded the engineers to reverse their recommendation. The next day, 73 seconds after lift-off, the shuttle was engulfed in a fireball, disintegrated and crashed into the sea. All those on board were killed.[7]

Subsequent studies[8] found that NASA's corporate culture strongly discouraged dissent. Managers were so focused on their goal of ensuring that launches went ahead on schedule that corners were repeatedly cut and safety advice ignored. Even more crucially, information about safety warnings was not passed up through the chain of command. When he gave the final go-ahead for the ill-fated launch, Jesse Moore, the man with ultimate responsibility for the mission, had no idea that engineers lower down the chain had raised any concerns.[9]

The term 'groupthink' was popularised in the 1970s by the American psychologist Irving Janis, whose initial focus was his country's foreign policy failures of the previous decade. Janis had been puzzled by President Kennedy's decision to back a fatally flawed CIA plan to invade Cuba in the hope of triggering a popular uprising.[10] The 1961 'Bay of Pigs' invasion was a disaster, with hundreds of the CIA-trained Cuban exiles involved in the attack being either captured or killed.

Flawed intelligence had led the CIA to believe that Cubans would welcome the invasion, and join the armed struggle against Fidel Castro's communist government.

But it later became clear that Castro enjoyed widespread popular support[11] – and that many of those who disagreed were languishing in prison and thus unable to be of much help to the would-be liberators. In the face of any counter-attack, the invaders were supposed to retreat to the mountains and begin a guerrilla campaign – but to do so they would have needed to cross 80 miles of swampland.[12]

An integral part of the plan was the launching by the US of pre-emptive bombing raids to eliminate the Cuban air force on the ground. For political reasons, it was decided this should be done covertly. In order to ensure 'deniability', the US chose to deploy a small group of ageing Second World War bombers, repainted to look like Cuban planes.[13] But the first air strike was unsuccessful, and – predictably perhaps – photos of the repainted planes quickly became public. Kennedy then cancelled the second air strike, even though the invasion was already under way. The 1,000 or so exiles could do little to defend themselves as a largely undamaged Cuban air force bombed and strafed them on the beaches, and a force of 20,000 ground troops advanced to repel them. Within 24 hours it was all over.[14]

Kennedy and his advisers had failed to take seriously the gaping holes in the plan, argues Irving Janis, because their desire for unanimity had overridden their ability, as a group, to make rational decisions.[15] This, for Janis, is the defining feature of groupthink. The problem was not so much that the group members were sycophants and fakers who would say anything to please the president – it was more that they were genuinely so close on a personal level that individual members were afraid of upsetting each other if they voiced their professional concerns too strongly. Supporting the consensus view was equated with loyalty, and loyalty to the group had started to seem more important than the need to voice doubts openly and honestly.

Irving Janis identifies eight 'symptoms' of groupthink, most or all of which were present in the case studies he looked at. These include:

1. Illusions of invulnerability, leading to unjustified optimism and excessive risk-taking – 'everything is going to work out all right, because we are a special group';
2. Rationalisation – explaining away warnings that challenge the group's assumptions;
3. Unquestioning belief in the morality of the group; ignoring the negative moral consequences of group decisions;
4. Stereotyping of those who oppose the group's view as weak, evil, impotent or stupid;
5. Direct pressure being placed on any member who questions the group, couched in terms of 'disloyalty';
6. Self-censorship of ideas that stray from the apparent consensus;
7. The illusion of unanimity among group members, with silence being viewed as agreement;

8. Self-appointed 'mindguards' within the group who screen out and suppress dissenting information.[16]

We see a number of these symptoms at work in the experience of Arthur Schlesinger, one of the few people within Kennedy's circle who did raise doubts about the wisdom of the Bay of Pigs invasion. Lacking the confidence to speak out in an open meeting, he expressed his concerns via a series of written memos to the president – but these did nothing to change the course of events.

'In the months after the Bay of Pigs I bitterly reproached myself for having kept so silent during those crucial discussions in the cabinet room', Schlesinger later wrote. 'I can only explain my failure to do more than raise a few timid questions by reporting that one's impulse to blow the whistle on this nonsense was simply undone by the circumstances of the discussion ... It is one thing for a Special Assistant to talk frankly in private to a President at his request, and another for a college professor, fresh to the government, to interpose his unassisted judgement in open meeting against that of such august figures as the Secretaries of State and Defense and the Joint Chiefs of Staff.'[17]

In addition to the fear of being in conflict with major figures of authority, Schlesinger was also pressured directly by the attorney general, Robert Kennedy – the president's own brother – to keep his thoughts to himself. 'Don't push it any further', the younger Kennedy insisted. The president had already made up his mind. Furthermore, says Schlesinger, 'advocates of the adventure had a rhetorical advantage. They could strike virile poses and talk of tangible things – firepower, air strike, landing craft and so on. To oppose the plan, one had to invoke intangibles – the moral position of the United States, the reputation of the President, the response of the United Nations, "world opinion" and other such odious concepts.'

The tragedies of the *Challenger* disaster and the Bay of Pigs show some of the deadly consequences of groupthink. At the extreme, there is almost no limit to the damage that can be done. Irving Janis has argued that groupthink also played a crucial rule in the US decision to escalate its involvement in the Indochina war, which claimed 58,000 US lives and killed up to 3 million Vietnamese.[18] Earlier in this book we saw how, in communist China during the late 1950s, a dogmatic adherence to pseudoscientific ideas about agriculture, coupled with groupthink within the circle of advisers around Chairman Mao, helped to create a famine which claimed tens of millions of lives.

But you don't have to be in charge of a space programme or a peasant revolution to be susceptible to groupthink, and for that to be a problem. Many of us will find ourselves, at one time or another, being asked by colleagues to endorse a course of action that seems manifestly unethical or reckless. A school or college may knowingly distort exam results in order to disguise its failure to meet official targets. A business may risk criminal prosecution by making false claims about the benefits of its products. Government agencies may expose the public to identity fraud by cutting corners in the protection of confidential personal data. Charities and political parties may expose themselves to damaging publicity by accepting 'dodgy' donations. And all of these things may take place amid a culture of wishful thinking and rationalisation: 'It's for the good of the organisation ... This comes from the top ... No-one will ever find out ... Everyone else is doing it too ... This is the way we've always done it.'

As Charlie Skelton found out on board '*Earth Orbiter One*', when those close to you are in the grip of a powerful delusion, it can be difficult to resist being sucked in – even when you know, rationally, that it's completely nonsensical. But in the real world, as many have found to their cost, the path of least resistance can sometimes prove more troublesome and expensive, in the long run, than taking a deep breath and speaking out.

CHAPTER TEN

'AIDS PROPHETS'
AND 'HIV VOODOO PRIESTS'

Little by little my health improved. I slowly gained weight and as I became better I began some sessions of acupuncture, osteopathy and went to my prayer group twice a month. I continued to have long talks with my homeopath, who was my greatest moral support ... In April 1996 I came across the work of Mark Griffiths ... What a relief it was to meet people who are there and approachable and to no longer be alone facing the trauma and fear of AIDS. Thanks to him I have been able to throw my last fears in the bin and to realize that I had struggled for ten years against a virus that does not exist! Today, thank heaven, I have discovered a marvellous life. AIDS has allowed me to connect with my deepest instincts and the word 'faith' has now taken on its true dimension.

Sylvie Cousseau, 'My Leap of Faith', *Continuum* magazine, spring 1998[1]

The contagious, HIV hypothesis of AIDS is the biggest scientific, medical blunder of the 20th century. The evidence is overwhelming that AIDS is not contagious,

> *sexually transmitted, or caused by HIV… The physi-*
> *cians who know or suspect the truth are embarrassed*
> *or afraid to admit that the HIV tests are absurd and*
> *should be outlawed, and that the anti-HIV drugs are*
> *injuring and killing people …*
>
> David Rasnick, 'The AIDS Blunder', *Mail and*
> *Guardian* (South Africa), 2001[2]

There's a myth around 'alternative medicine' that goes something like this: mainstream science claims a monopoly on medical treatment and dismisses other, more traditional – or unconventional – forms of medicine, which are different, yet equally valid. Modern medical science is tech-nocratic rather than traditional, reductionist rather than 'holistic', industrial rather than organic, commercial rather than communal. 'Alternative medicine' represents a gentler, more inclusive approach, drawing on the ancient wisdom and traditions of non-Western cultures, and treating the patient as a whole rather than focusing only on the most obvious manifestations of sickness. But due to the power of the medical profession and the pharmaceutical industry, and the dogmatic 'Western' ideology of mainstream science, this alternative approach is suppressed and excluded.

Like all good myths, the myth of alternative medicine has many grains of truth. Hospitals are often big, scary and impersonal. Doctors can seem arrogant and bossy. Pharmaceutical companies are in business, first and foremost, to make money. Modern medicine – with its needles and pills, scalpels, stitches and chemical smells – often feels cold, invasive, alien and detached from tradition. Every so often, things go horribly wrong, and a doctor ends up killing or maiming a patient rather than curing them. And every so often new medical treatments do come along – or old ones are revisited – which are accepted into the mainstream, having once been viewed with suspicion.

The myth of alternative medicine plays to a very real yearning for more humanity within medicine, and the self-evident conviction that science hasn't yet found all the answers to our health problems. At the moderate end, advocates of alternative medicine can seem reasonable, tolerant and modern. But at the extreme, they can start to sound like the peddlers of dangerous conspiracy theories. And few such theories are more dangerous than the denialism that has grown up around HIV and Aids.

In 1981, the Center for Disease Control in the US identified a significant rise in pneumonia deaths among previously healthy gay men, whose immune systems had suffered catastrophic collapse. By the end of the year, the phenomenon had been given a name – Acquired Immune Deficiency Syndrome, or Aids. In May 1983, scientists working at the Pasteur Institute in Paris announced the discovery of a new virus that they believed to be the cause of the disease. The discovery was confirmed by US scientists the following year.

But not everyone was convinced. In an article in *The Journal of Psychohistory* in 1984, the psychiatrist Caspar

Schmidt proposed that Aids was the product not of a virus but of a self-hating 'group fantasy' among gay men, drug addicts and other minority groups. A 'vast, society-wide conservative swing' from 1977 onwards had led to an 'epidemic of shame-induced depression' among these groups. The immune system collapse observed in Aids sufferers was a 'psychogenically' induced product of this depression, Schmidt argued. 'One can only hope, for the sake of the 2,500 people in the United States living with a diagnosis of Aids, and the 90-odd who are newly diagnosed each week, that we wake up from the trance, and soon.'[3]

And yet the figures continued to grow. In 1985 there were more than 12,000 new cases and nearly 7,000 deaths in the USA alone[4] – an increasing number of them among heterosexuals who had never abused drugs. That year, US trials of the drug azidothymidine (AZT) showed that it could help slow the progress of Aids. By 1987, AZT had been officially licensed as a treatment for the disease.[5] But the drug could still do little but delay the inevitable – although patients were living a little longer, the death toll kept rising; more than 1,000 people were now dying from Aids every month.[6]

1987 saw the launch of public health campaigns in a number of countries around the world. 'Don't die of ignorance', Britons were urged, in government leaflets issued to every household in the country.[7] But that same year Peter Duesberg, an eminent US virologist, began publicly questioning the growing international consensus. Unlike Caspar Schmidt, Duesberg acknowledged the existence of HIV –

but he maintained that the virus was harmless.[8]

Like Clarence Cook Little's objections to the theory linking smoking and cancer, Duesberg's denial of the HIV–Aids hypothesis rested on uncertainties about the precise mechanism by which the virus could cause disease, rather than any experiments that he himself had done. Few of his peers were convinced, pointing to the growing epidemiological and experimental data linking Aids and HIV. But Duesberg persisted, arguing that the illness was more likely to be caused by recreational drug use, and that AZT – the first drug to be used in treating Aids – was itself a 'poison'.[9]

While Duesberg gained few converts among his fellow scientists, he enjoyed widespread media coverage and won vocal support among some Aids activists. Many in the American gay community were still instinctively distrustful of the country's medical establishment, which had classified homosexuality as a mental illness until the early 1970s.[10] There was also considerable disquiet about the side effects of AZT, which were often severe, and about the establishment's failure to produce a more effective treatment.

Duesberg's cause was taken up by the gay rights activist John Lauritsen, in a series of articles for the *New York Native* magazine. Lauritsen supported Duesberg's 'alternative hypothesis' that Aids was caused by recreational drugs, particularly amyl nitrate – commonly known as 'poppers' – which was used widely in the gay community. Lauritsen also shared Duesberg's concerns about AZT. In 1990, Lauritsen published a book, *Poison by Prescription*, with a foreword by Duesberg, in which he argued that AZT was 'a deadly drug', approved on the basis of 'fraudulent research'.[11] The following year, Lauritsen, Duesberg and a long list of others, including some well-respected scientists, signed an open letter calling for the 'reappraisal of the HIV/Aids hypothesis',[12] and submitted it to four major scientific journals. But the views on which the letter was based were becoming increasingly discredited, and the journals refused to publish it.

Duesberg and his supporters seized on their marginalisation as evidence that dissident views were being suppressed by the scientific community for political reasons. Throughout the early 1990s, the 'Aids dissidents' successfully gained coverage in the mainstream media by capitalising on their exclusion from mainstream science.

'In a deathly conspiracy of silence', wrote Celia Farber for the cult music magazine, *Spin,* in 1992, 'the medical establishment is ignoring powerful evidence that HIV doesn't spread sexually, and it may in fact be harmless'.[13]

'They call HIV the Aids virus, and it's this generation's symbol of terror. It has come to rule us, our lives, our relationships, our sexuality ...' Farber declared, echoing Caspar Schmidt's view of Aids as a self-hating group fantasy. 'We have erected buildings, organizations, conferences, and global programs in an attempt to placate it. It is a demon, and we worship it with our terror.' In 1993, John Lauritsen published an apocalyptic book, *The AIDS War*, which denounced the 'propaganda, profiteering and genocide' of the 'medical-industrial complex', and claimed that the medical establishment was knowingly poisoning tens of thousands of people.[14]

In the UK, Duesberg's views were championed by Neville Hodgkinson, the *Sunday Times* medical correspondent. 'A kind of collective insanity over HIV and Aids has gripped leaders of the scientific and medical professions', he wrote in 1994. 'They have stopped behaving as scientists, and instead are working as propagandists, trying desperately to keep alive a failed theory.'[15]

But while Farber's 'conspiracy of silence' and Hodgkinson's 'collective insanity' made for good copy, a three-month investigation by the journal *Science* suggested a more prosaic explanation for the exclusion of the Aids dissidents. Mainstream researchers accused Duesberg of constructing his arguments by 'selective reading of the scientific literature, dismissing evidence that contradicts his theses, requiring impossibly definitive proof, and dismissing outright studies marked by inconsequential weaknesses'.[16] Duesberg had crossed the line from science into pseudoscience.

In the first few years of the Aids epidemic, very little research had been done on the nature and extent of the disease, and there were still many gaps in the mainstream account of how it was caused. But by the early 1990s many of these gaps had been filled, and a growing body of evidence, published in peer-reviewed scientific journals, was showing a close correlation between HIV infection and Aids. One among many such studies was published in *The Lancet* in 1993. Researchers had followed the progress of 715 gay men over a median average of 8.6 years. Of the 136 Aids cases that developed during this time, all occurred among the 365 men who had been HIV-positive at the start of the study.[17] None occurred in the men who had tested negative for HIV, even though many reported engaging in the 'risk behaviours' that Duesberg believed caused Aids. In the same year, the Center for Disease Control in the US published the results of a review of 230,179 Aids-like cases reported since the very beginning of the epidemic. Where an HIV test had been carried out, more than 99 per cent had tested positive. Only 47 patients with an unexplained severe immune deficiency had tested negative for HIV.[18]

Although there were clear signs that intravenous drug users faced a higher risk of HIV transmission than non-users, not a single study could find evidence to support Duesberg's hypothesis that Aids was caused by drugs. The connection between HIV and Aids was further strengthened by the fact that AZT, then the sole therapy with a proven record of slowing the disease, was a drug that worked by targeting the virus directly. There was no evidence to support Duesberg's claim that AZT itself could cause Aids.

Peter Duesberg's admirers have compared him to Galileo,[19] the 17th-century astronomer whose observations with an early telescope led him to reject the view, dominant at the time – and supported by the Catholic Church – that the Earth was the centre of the universe. Galileo was branded a heretic by the Inquisition, his writings were banned, he was forced to recant what he had written, and he was placed under house arrest for the remainder of his life. Aids 'dissidents' have compared this treatment with Duesberg's loss of credibility among scientists, and the refusal of some scientific journals to publish his work. But what marked Galileo out as a scientist was not his opposition to the establishment per se, but rather his willingness to question that established dogma on the basis of hard evidence. As the science writer Robert Park reputedly once said: 'To wear the mantle of Galileo it is not enough that you be persecuted by an unkind establishment, you must also be right.'[20]

Peter Duesberg arguably has less in common with Galileo than with the theologians who insisted that Galileo's observations with the telescope must be wrong – some suggested that they were illusions created by demons – because they contradicted the established cosmology of the Catholic Church. Duesberg's insistence that HIV was harmless stemmed not from any experimental research that he or anybody else had done, but rather from his theoretical views about the nature of viruses and retroviruses. Rather than trying to modify his theories in the face of data that clearly suggested that HIV is the cause of a deadly disease, Duesberg chose instead to reject that data. To many of Duesberg's supporters, however, the criticisms made by his fellow scientists were merely further evidence of the power of the conspirators.

In the *Sunday Times*, alongside Duesberg and other self-described 'dissidents', Neville Hodgkinson interviewed a number of HIV patients who had chosen not to take anti-retrovirals. Among them was Jody Wells, who had been HIV-positive since 1984 and diagnosed with Aids two years later. 'Today, seven years on, he says he feels fine with energy levels that belie his 52 years', Hodgkinson reported in 1993.[21]

Jody Wells was the founder and editor-in-chief of the London-based magazine *Continuum*, which worked to challenge the 'orthodox view' of Aids and HIV. Operating from a small office in London's trendy Brunswick Centre, Wells' magazine questioned the existence of HIV, denied that Aids could be sexually transmitted, promoted Caspar Schmidt's view of Aids as 'psychogenically' induced, and emphasised 'nutritional and lifestyle approaches' rather than drug therapies.

Hodgkinson's articles on HIV–Aids exposed the *Sunday Times* to sustained criticism from mainstream scientists, and he left the newspaper in 1994. But as the 'Aids reappraisal' movement lost ground in the mainstream media, the 'dissidents' were quick to seize the opportunities presented by the internet. 1996 saw the launch of Virusmyth.net, taking the fight onto the world wide web. Other websites soon followed, reproducing 'Aids dissident' articles from the mainstream media alongside their own original content.

But the movement was beginning to face a serious crisis: many of the HIV-positive 'dissidents' who refused Aids medications were themselves beginning to develop the disease and die. In 1994, the psychologist Caspar Schmidt succumbed to an Aids-related illness. The following year saw the death of *Continuum* magazine's editor, Jody Wells.[22]

Meanwhile, a new generation of antiretroviral drugs seemed at last to be offering real hope to those living with HIV. In 1997, for the first time since the epidemic began, US deaths from Aids fell significantly – from more than 38,000 in 1996 to just over 21,000.[23] This coincided directly with widespread distribution of the new generation of antiretroviral drugs – and there were dramatic reports of Aids patients being pulled back from the brink of death by the latest therapy.

Following the death of Jody Wells, *Continuum* magazine's new editor Huw Christie defiantly announced the 'Jody Wells memorial prize', offering £1,000 to anyone who could prove to the magazine's satisfaction that HIV was real. The magazine poured scorn on the new antiretroviral drugs, highlighting cases of Aids activists who had used them and subsequently died. In every issue, the magazine ran a column entitled 'Lust For Life', profiling people with HIV who had chosen not to take antiretroviral drugs. One such contributor was Sylvie Cousseau, whose words were quoted at the beginning of this chapter. Her partner Mark Griffiths also gave his own testimony, emphasising that 'illness is caused by a breakdown in communication ... becoming disconnected with our "soul", our very source ... In the light of self-discovery and research into the fundamental similarities in the self-healing approach of fellow survivors, I discovered a positive holistic approach'.

Looking through old editions of *Continuum* magazine, many of which are still available online,[24] it is hard not to be drawn in by the passion and eloquence of the writing. Huw Christie, Michael Baumgartner and their fellow writers speak with an authoritative voice, wielding with apparent ease the complex scientific terminology of HIV and Aids as they highlight perceived flaws in the 'established' theory.

Buzzwords abound, from 'contrasting paradigms' to 'challenging the orthodoxy' and the 'Western model of medicine'. Every variation of 'Aids reappraisal' is explored. HIV is psychoanalysed away as a 'mass illusion' and a 'group fantasy'. Doctors and scientists are 'puritans', 'propagandists', 'Aids prophets' and 'HIV voodoo priests' seeking to impose their creed on the gay community. Aids deaths are attributed not to a virus but to a 'manic lifestyle' or AZT, or the stress of having to live with the 'label' of being HIV-positive. Readers are directed to the writings of the postmodernist thinkers Michel Foucault and Paul Feyerabend, and given detailed advice on 'natural alternatives' to antiretroviral drugs. Peter Duesberg, John Lauritsen, David Rasnick, Neville Hodgkinson and other leading 'dissidents' all appear as guest contributors.

But it's hard, too, to avoid being struck by a sense of poignancy. Some of those who wrote for *Continuum* magazine continue to make their arguments today on the ever-growing number of 'Aids reappraisal' websites scattered across the internet. But many more of these eloquent voices have now fallen silent. In October 2000, *Continuum*'s editor Huw Christie, like Jody Wells before him, became seriously ill. The following August he died, aged just 41, and the magazine ceased publication.

'Neither of your illnesses would have brought you down, Huw',[25] wrote his friend and fellow campaigner Michael Baumgartner in a tribute on the Virusmyth website. 'You simply ran out of time to change gear. We both knew it did not need some ill-identified virus to explain your several symptoms ... Poverty had taken its toll, and so had the no-future urban gay lifestyle you had in common with so many other gay men, especially in cities like London.'

2001 also saw the early death of Sylvie Cousseau, the *Continuum* contributor who had refused antiretroviral drugs, and thought that she could treat Aids with acupuncture and homeopathy. Her partner, Mark Griffiths, claimed that her death was due to cancer. Three years later, Griffiths himself died. 'Dissident' friends insisted that his passing was 'non-Aids related', and blamed alcohol and antibiotics.[26]

The argument about the link between HIV and Aids has many parallels with the debate around smoking and lung cancer. Like Clarence Cook Little, Peter Duesberg set an impossibly high standard of 'proof' for the theory he was disputing – whilst setting the bar much lower for the alternative explanation. Like Little, Duesberg was highly selective in the evidence that he chose to accept or ignore. As with smoking and cancer during the 1960s, journalists sympathetic to 'Aids reappraisal' sought to characterise the link between HIV and Aids as a matter of 'scientific controversy', even though the scientists whose views they championed represented a small, marginalised minority. And also as with smoking and cancer, many mainstream journalists were drawn in, feeling obliged to tell 'both sides of the story'.

Yet there are also many differences. The pseudoscience over smoking and cancer was part of a multi-million-dollar campaign, funded by a powerful multinational industry and finessed by the best PR machine that money could buy. There was no such power behind the cause of 'Aids reappraisal'. Many 'dissidents' operated on a shoestring budget – some had given up lucrative careers to pursue their campaign. While smoking–cancer 'sceptics' tried to play down the extent of the scientific consensus on the issue they were contesting, the fake 'sceptics' of HIV–Aids often sought to highlight it as evidence of the power of the conspiracy that was ranged against them. While Clarence Cook Little described himself as an 'ultraconservative' within science, the dissidents sought to define themselves by their opposition to the 'established orthodoxy'.

And whereas the motivation behind the pseudoscience around smoking and cancer appears fairly straightforward, the driving force behind 'Aids reappraisal' seems far harder to understand. Jody Wells, Huw Christie, Sylvie Cousseau and Mark Griffiths are just a few names in a grim roll-call of vocal, HIV-positive 'Aids dissidents' who believed so strongly in their cause that they refused to take medicines that could have saved their lives.

Identifying a flawed argument is usually much easier than psychoanalysing the motivations of the person making it. But what does seem noticeable is that many of the dyed-in-the-wool Aids denialists who eventually succumbed to the disease had received their HIV diagnosis in the mid-to-late 1980s, long before there was any real prospect of effective treatment. For some, denying the existence of Aids may have been a way to stave off the painful knowledge that they had an incurable disease that was likely to kill them within a few years.

'I was already looking for a way out, something that meant I wasn't inevitably going to die', says Winstone Zulu, an HIV-positive activist who was diagnosed in 1990 and became an 'Aids dissident' in the late 1990s. 'So here were these people saying, "It's all been this vast mistake. It's not what causes Aids." Looking back, I think it was about wishing Aids away.'[27]

Being an 'Aids dissident' was, Zulu says, 'like printing money when the economy is not doing well. Or pissing in your pants when the weather is too cold. Comforting for a while but disastrous in the long run.'[28]

Zulu became severely ill in 2001, after 'Aids dissident' friends had persuaded him to stop taking his medications. But when he began taking them again, his health improved dramatically. Unlike so many others, Winstone Zulu lived to tell the tale. He now campaigns publicly against what he calls 'Aids denialism'.

Aids denial and bogus scepticism

As we saw earlier, those seeking to advance a pseudoscientific theory – be it about smoking, asbestos or the Holocaust – will often seek to appropriate the language of scepticism, and characterise themselves as no-nonsense 'debunkers', even while they give credence to a highly tenuous alternative explanation. While the self-described 'Aids sceptics' dismiss the mountain of research linking HIV and Aids, they are prepared to believe, on the basis of weak or non-existent evidence, that the massive immune system damage seen in Aids patients could be caused by drug use, stress or a 'manic lifestyle'.

Another giveaway sign is the use of a conspiracy theory to explain why the 'establishment' has got it so disastrously wrong. In the world of David Rasnick, the association between HIV and Aids is the 'biggest scientific ... blunder of the 20th century', and this fact is being covered up by the pharmaceutical industry, along with the clinicians who know the truth but are too 'embarrassed or afraid' to admit it.[29] To John Lauritsen, Aids is a 'myth' perpetrated by the 'medical-industrial complex',[30] whose 'toxic' drugs are causing death and destruction on a 'genocidal' scale.

A related tactic is attempting to explain away the consensus in vague psychological or sociological terms. For Caspar Schmidt, Aids was the result of a 'group delusion', and a typical example of 'epidemic hysteria'. For John Lauritsen, the disease was not only a conspiracy but also a 'religion' and a 'death cult'.[31] For the denialist Ian Young, Aids was a product of 'the group fantasy of the Homosexual as doomed Grotesque'. The HIV test was a ritual 'rite of passage' for young gay men, and the taking of antiretroviral drugs was akin to 'holy communion', and 'an act of faith and obedience guaranteeing salvation'.[32]

As with conspiracy theories, the defining feature of these arguments is the lack of concrete evidence to back them up. While there is evidence that a mental disorder can produce some physiological effects, Caspar Schmidt's conviction that psychological factors alone were responsible for the enormous immune damage seen in Aids patients – and the thousands of deaths that resulted – was wildly speculative. Likewise, Ian Young offered no evidence to support his claim that the primary motivation for those who chose to take Aids medications was spiritual relief or social conformity, rather than the simple expectation that these drugs would help to prolong their lives.

The authority of any scientific theory ultimately rests on the claim that the theory is grounded in a rational and objective evaluation of the hard evidence. By characterising the mainstream scientific view as akin to a religion, denialists seek to undermine this authority by asserting or implying that the theory is based not on evidence but on faith, or dogma. This characterisation is further emphasised by describing the mainstream theory as an 'orthodoxy', with those who have the courage to 'challenge the orthodoxy' being persecuted as 'heretics'.

Perhaps the most famous exponent of this view of the HIV–Aids debate is President Thabo Mbeki of South Africa, who outlined his concerns in a letter to his fellow world leaders in April 2000:

> People who otherwise would fight very hard to defend the critically important rights of freedom of thought and speech occupy, with regard to the HIV–AIDS issue, the frontline in the campaign of intellectual intimidation and terrorism which argues that the only freedom we have is to agree with what they decree to be established scientific truths. Some agitate for these extraordinary propositions with a religious fervour born by a degree of fanaticism, which is truly frightening. The day may not be far off when we will, once again, see books burnt and their authors immolated by fire by those who believe that they have a duty to conduct a holy crusade against the infidels.[33]

In Europe and the US, where the pseudoscience of Aids denialism has been nurtured and developed over two decades, it has nonetheless remained a minority view: dangerous, no doubt, to the few who subscribe to it, yet largely marginalised within the mainstream. But in South Africa, where Aids has now reached a pandemic scale, the ideas of the 'Aids dissidents' have had a direct impact on public policy. The next section will look at what happens when a denialist conspiracy theory is taken into the heart of government.

CHAPTER ELEVEN

CAN A VIRUS CAUSE
A SYNDROME?

In 1997 Olga Visser, a South African hospital technician, claimed dramatic success in unlicensed trials of her drug 'Virodene', offering hope of a cheap, effective and authentically 'African' treatment for Aids. Olga and her businessman husband Zigi spoke so convincingly that health minister Nkosazana Zuma invited them to present their findings to members of the ANC cabinet, including the then-deputy president, Thabo Mbeki. The Vissers testified that Virodene could fight HIV 'in areas other drugs cannot reach',[1] and produced several Aids patients who reported near-miraculous improvements in their health.

'It was like a church confessional', one member of the presidential staff later reported. 'The patients said they were dying, they got this treatment, and then they were saved! The thing I will always remember is the pride in South African scientists.'[2]

Ministers were impressed, and agreed to look favourably at the Vissers' request for government funding. But the country's Medicines Control Council (MCC) was more sceptical. The Vissers had conducted medical tests on human beings without any of the standard procedures –

there had been no animal trials, no prior experiments to test the drug for possible toxicity, and there was no 'placebo' control group against which the results could be compared. The Vissers' attempts to explain how the drug was working were riddled with basic misunderstandings and inaccuracies. Most worrying of all, Virodene was found to contain a known industrial solvent, dimethylformamide – a common ingredient in paint-stripper – which could cause liver damage if ingested. The MCC ruled that all further tests on humans should be halted until these concerns had been addressed.

Zigi Visser reportedly claimed that the MCC had acted under 'under pressure from the established Aids research groups',[3] and the ANC secretary general, Kgalema Motlanthe, echoed this view. Deputy President Mbeki publicly criticised the MCC for its refusal to allow the resumption of human tests. Health Minister Zuma lobbied the chair of the MCC, Peter Folb, to reverse his decision.

In March 1998, Folb was removed from his post and replaced.[4] But to the government's dismay, his successor was no more willing to wave through the tests that they were demanding, and a series of independent reviews endorsed the MCC's conclusions. The Vissers were unperturbed, and sought to run the trials overseas. They continued to receive support from an ANC leadership determined to find an alternative to Western-produced Aids drugs.

The ANC's suspicion of their country's white-dominated scientific establishment was in many ways understandable. The complicity of white medics and scientists with the apartheid regime was well-documented, and some still retained the positions they had held under the old regime. In 1997 Daan Goosen, a former government scientist who had headed a military research laboratory, gave a testimony to the post-apartheid 'Truth and Reconciliation Commission' that made some conspiracy theories look positively mild. Goosen revealed that the apartheid government had asked him to look into producing a germ warfare weapon capable of killing black South Africans – or rendering them infertile – while leaving whites unharmed.[5] Peter Folb himself had testified before the same commission as an expert witness on the complicity of white doctors in the death of the anti-apartheid activist Steve Biko.

In October 1998, Health Minister Zuma called a halt to trials of the drug AZT among HIV-positive pregnant women, claiming that they were not 'cost effective'.[6] The move was criticised by health professionals and by the South African media, but Anthony Brink, a Pietermaritzburg barrister, applauded the decision. In an article published the following March, Brink issued a colourful denunciation of AZT, citing Peter Duesberg, John Lauritsen and a number of other Aids 'dissidents'. Brink claimed that the drug was a 'medicine from hell',[7] approved on fraudulent grounds, and that it was killing HIV patients.

The Vissers seized on Brink's article and sent copies to Mbeki and Zuma, together with a 30,000-word tract in which Brink expounded his views in more detail. Mbeki, who had now taken over the presidency following the retirement of Nelson Mandela, was sufficiently impressed to refer to Brink's claims in a speech to a meeting in Cape Town, in October 1999:

> There are legal cases pending in this country, the United Kingdom and the United States against AZT on the basis that this drug is harmful to health. There exists a large volume of scientific literature alleging that, among other things, the toxicity of this drug is such that it is in fact a danger to health … These are matters of great concern to the Government as it would be irresponsible for us not to head the dire warnings which medical researchers have been making.[8]

Mbeki later reported that it was Brink's writings that had first introduced him to the work of the Aids 'dissidents'. Over the next few months, he immersed himself in denialist literature. Early in 2000, Mbeki contacted the US denialist David Rasnick and subsequently invited him, along with a number of his fellow 'dissidents', to join a presidential 'Advisory Panel' on Aids and HIV. When quizzed by the media, the president's spokesman Parks Mankahlana explained that the purpose of the panel would be to examine 'everything about Aids', from antiretroviral drugs to 'whether there's this thing called AIDS … whether HIV leads to AIDS, whether there is something called HIV'.[9]

The dissidents had finally succeeded in convincing a major establishment figure that the link between Aids and HIV was a matter of scientific 'controversy'. Fifteen years after that link was first discovered, during which time millions had died, scientists were called upon to investigate whether the disease even existed. Those invited to South Africa included Peter Duesberg, who denied that HIV caused Aids, Eleni Papadopulos-Eleopolus, who denied that HIV existed, and David Rasnick, who believed that HIV testing should be outlawed and antiretroviral treatments stopped.[10] Also in attendance were Neville Hodgkinson,[11] who as a *Sunday Times* science correspondent had alleged a 'conspiracy of silence' around HIV and who subsequently wrote a book describing it as 'a virus that never was', Huw Christie of *Continuum* magazine,[12] who had put up a £1,000 prize for anyone who could prove to him that HIV was real, and Celia Farber,[13] who believed that there was 'powerful evidence that HIV doesn't spread sexually, and it may in fact be harmless'.

The outrage that Mbeki's approach was causing among local doctors, clinicians and Aids activists was merely taken as further proof of the strength of the 'myth' and the power of the vested interests ranged behind it. 'The tragedy is that HIV/Aids is not going to succumb to the machinations of the profiteering pharmaceutical companies and their propagandists', wrote presidential spokesman Mankahlana in March 2000. 'Like the marauders of the military industrial complex who propagated fear to increase their profits, the profit-takers ... benefiting from the scourge of HIV/Aids will disappear to the affluent beaches of the world to enjoy wealth accumulated from a humankind ravaged by a dreaded disease.'[14]

While the ANC leadership sought to tackle the 'profiteering' of pharmaceutical companies by embracing Aids denialism, South African Aids activists were pursuing a different tack. By the spring of 2000, several of the big pharmaceutical companies had agreed, under heavy pressure from the high-profile 'Treatment Action Campaign', to supply Aids drugs at a fraction of the price charged in Europe and the US. Aids activists were exuberant, but when civil society leaders wrote to Mbeki asking him to reconsider his position on AZT, the response was churlish. The president announced that he was taken aback 'by the determination of many people in our country to sacrifice all intellectual integrity to act as salespersons of the product of one pharmaceutical company'.

The acrimonious presidential panel meetings between the 'dissenters' and the mainstream scientists did little to resolve the disagreements between them. Ignoring all the evidence that they were shown about the link between Aids and HIV, and the benefits of antiretroviral treatment, the denialists stuck resolutely to the position that 'Aids would disappear instantaneously'[15] if HIV tests were outlawed and the use of antiretroviral drugs terminated. Mbeki's willingness to take the denialists seriously was seen by his peers as naive, rather than visionary and open-minded.

At the July 2000 international Aids conference in Durban, delegates were astonished by Mbeki's position. By the end of the conference, 5,000 scientists from around the world had signed the 'Durban Declaration', affirming that the evidence linking HIV and Aids was 'clear-cut, exhaustive and unambiguous'. Mbeki's new health minister, Manto Tshabalala-Msimang, condemned the statement as 'elitist'.

In September of the same year, a row erupted after Tshabalala-Msimang circulated a copy of a chapter from a book which claimed that Aids was the result of a conspiracy between space aliens and a shadowy and secretive global clique known as the 'Illuminati'.[16] Later that month, Mbeki confirmed that government health programmes continued to be based on the 'premise' that HIV caused Aids, but went on to ask: 'Does HIV cause Aids? Can a virus cause a syndrome? How? It can't, because a syndrome is a group of diseases resulting from acquired immune deficiency'.[17] He then told a closed ANC meeting that the CIA was working covertly to undermine him and his government, because his questioning of the link between HIV and Aids was jeopardising drug company profits.[18]

Soon afterwards, it was announced that Mbeki was 'withdrawing' from the public debate about HIV and Aids. But within days, his office issued a statement claiming that 'our people are being used as guinea pigs and conned into using dangerous and toxic drugs', and that this was 'reminiscent of the biological warfare of the apartheid era'. Three days after that, on 26 October 2000, Mbeki's spokesman Parks Mankahlana died suddenly, aged 36, from a mysterious illness.[19] The president refused to comment on rumours that this illness was Aids.

Prices of antiretroviral drugs, meanwhile, were continuing to fall, with some manufacturers even offering to provide them to South Africa for free. Yet the government steadfastly held out against pressure to make them available, claiming ongoing concerns about whether the drugs were safe. In response, Aids activists began a series of high-profile court cases to compel the government to give patients access to the medicines they needed.

The Virodene saga, meanwhile, was turning into a fiasco. In the face of continued opposition from the South African Medicines Controls Council, Zigi Visser arranged a trial of the drug in Tanzania. But the Tanzanian National Institute of Medical Research declared the trials illegal, and in September 2001 Visser was ignominiously deported. 'Our work is top secret so I can't say much,' Visser reportedly told South Africa's *Mail and Guardian*, 'but large international pharmaceutical companies and elements of the media are afraid of Virodene.'[20]

The following month, President Mbeki made a speech widely interpreted as a veiled attack on the activists campaigning for wider access to Aids drugs. Without specifying anyone by name, Mbeki condemned those who 'take to the streets carrying their placards, to demand that because we are germ carriers, and human beings of a lower order that cannot subject its passions to reason, we must perforce adopt strange opinions, to save a depraved and diseased people from perishing from self-inflicted disease'. The Aids campaigners, Mbeki suggested, were 'convinced that we are but natural-born, promiscuous carriers of germs', and 'proclaim that our continent is doomed to an inevitable mortal end because of our unconquerable devotion to the sin of lust'.[21]

Mbeki's attitude led to increasing divisions within his own party. In 2002, Nelson Mandela broke his silence, urging the government to stop blocking access to Aids medicines. 'If the government says, "don't make any move until we have completed our research", young people and babies are going to die in scores every day', he said in a speech at an Aids clinic in Soweto.[22] Later that year, Mandela made a point of meeting Zackie Achmat, the HIV-positive founder and chairman of the 'Treatment Action Campaign', which had campaigned relentlessly for greater public access to Aids medications.

Between 2001 and 2003, the Treatment Action Campaign won a series of legal victories, compelling the government to make antiretroviral drugs more widely available. But the government continued to drag its feet, and it was only in 2004 that they began to implement the court rulings.

Striking, too, was the extent to which members of the government continued to entertain denialist ideas, and make confusing statements over Aids, even after the state had been forced to change its policies. In 2003, health minister Tshabalala-Msimang earned worldwide ridicule after suggesting that Aids could be treated with 'African traditional remedies' such as beetroot, garlic and olive oil.

'These things are affordable for South Africans,' she told the media, 'not like things like antiretrovirals.'[23] Yet when the Global Fund for Aids donated $75 million to the South African province of KwaZulu-Natal to help buy life-saving medicines, the health minister blocked the distribution of the money, claiming that the grant application had been filed improperly.

The damage done by the influence of denialism was exacerbated by the ruling party's interference with the independent bodies who regulate medical treatment and trials. This has helped spur a proliferation of fake remedies and 'supplements' for Aids and other diseases. Virodene is just one of many false-hope cures that have appeared on the South African market in recent years.

In 2004, a German vitamin salesman, Matthias Rath, ran a series of newspaper adverts claiming that anti-retrovirals were 'poison', and urging Aids patients to stop using them in favour of the Dr Rath Foundation's 'natural' vitamin-based products. The following year it was revealed that Health Minister Manto Tsabalala-Msimang had held a private meeting with Rath, who claims that the 'Aids genocide' by the 'drug cartel' is part of a conspiracy by

Tony Blair and Gordon Brown to increase the profits of GlaxoSmithKline.

When challenged by opposition MPs, the health minister refused to distance herself from Rath's claims. When South Africa's main opposition party raised concerns about the unlicensed sale of 'fake cures', the government accused it of undermining 'indigenous knowledge' and perpetuating racial stereotypes. An inquiry into Matthias Rath by the Medicines Control Council stalled after the lead investigator was taken off the case.[24]

If Matthias Rath has added nothing of value to the fight against Aids itself, his contribution to the cause of Aids denialism is indisputable. Aided by Anthony Brink and David Rasnick, who now work for his 'Dr Rath Foundation', Rath has woven the many strands of half-truth, distortion, omission, conspiracy and hyperbole into a grand unifying theory of HIV denialism. In 2005, Rath issued what can only be described as a proclamation, declaring that:

> Never before in the history of mankind was a greater crime committed than the genocide organized by the pharmaceutical drug cartel in the interest of the multibillion-dollar investment business with disease. Hundreds of millions of people have died unnecessarily from Aids, cancer, heart disease and other preventable diseases and the only reason that these epidemics are still haunting mankind is that they

are the multibillion-dollar marketplace for the pharmaceutical drug cartel.[25]

Rath argues that the Aids epidemic in Africa is the product
of 'pharmaceutical colonialism', and accuses drug companies of using the continent as a 'testing ground and ...
multi-billion dollar market place for their controversial,
toxic – and often deadly – drugs'.

Pseudoscience, Aids denialism
and cultural relativism

In a stable, democratic society with strong, well-established political institutions, most conspiracy theories are
doubtless little more than harmless entertainment. But in
an emerging democracy struggling to overcome the legacy
of decades of racist injustice, conspiracy theorists who
play on long-standing divisions to spread their ideas can
have a devastating impact.

Aids denialism in South Africa was the product of an
extraordinary mix of politics, wishful thinking, cultural
antagonism, paranoia and cynical opportunism. Distrustful
both of their country's own medical establishment, and
of a global scientific community that they believed
embodied 'Western' values and interests, ANC leaders,
eager to make a mark for the new South Africa, were
willing to entertain ideas that no other government in the
world was taking seriously. Ignored and excluded in their

own countries, the likes of Matthias Rath, David Rasnick and Peter Duesberg grasped at the chance to advance their pet theories in a divided country, with little apparent regard for the consequences.

The South African government's dalliance with Aids denialism has fuelled one of the greatest man-made disasters of the modern era. By 2005, more than 5.5 million South Africans were infected with HIV, and 1,000 were dying from Aids every day. Between 1990 and 2006, life expectancy dropped by 20 per cent – from 64 years to just 51. Nicoli Natrass, an economist at the University of Cape Town, estimates that more than 340,000 deaths could have been prevented if the South African government had not deliberately delayed the roll-out of antiretroviral drugs.[26] This figure alone easily exceeds the 300,000 deaths caused by the decade-long civil war that ravaged Burundi during the 1990s, and the 200,000 killed in ethnic conflicts in the former Yugoslavia. It's difficult to know how many more South Africans have died after being persuaded to stop taking their medicines by the misinformation spread by Rasnick, Brink and Rath – and seemingly endorsed, in some cases, by their own government.

While the scale of South Africa's health disaster still falls short of the man-made famines of Maoist China and Soviet Russia, there are clear similarities between South Africa's state-endorsed Aids quackery and the Soviet pseudoscience of Trofim Lysenko. Where Lysenko dismissed his critics as 'bourgeois', South Africa's denialists sought to characterise mainstream Aids science as 'racist'. And as with Lysenko, the checks and balances that would normally protect the public from the worst effects of pseudoscience were systematically undermined by political interference and favouritism.

In South Africa, Aids denialism has appropriated the language of anti-colonial liberation, portraying science itself as inherently Western – both alien to South Africa's indigenous culture, and oppressive towards its people. Intertwined with this has been another characteristic feature of pseudoscience, the spurious appeal to relativism.

A document circulated among ANC offices in 2002 mused on 'HIV/AIDS and the Struggle for the Humanisation of the African', asserting that 'for centuries we have carried the burden of the crimes and falsities of "scientific" Eurocentrism, its dogmas imposed upon our being as the brands of a definitive, "universal" truth'.[27] Scientific objectivity was an 'illusion', the article claimed, and Aids science was the product of 'a racist world-view that coincides with the material self-interest of research institutions and of the Western governments that fund them ...' The war against Aids was 'also a war to defeat the humiliation and dehumanisation of the African people'.

Where Marxists sought to liberate humanity through the overthrow of the Western economic system, hard-line cultural relativists seek to overthrow the entire Western system of belief, from the philosophies of Ancient Greece to the rationalist ideals of the Enlightenment and – with increasing vehemence in recent years – the dominance of contemporary science.

Relativism in its most radical form asserts that there are no objective facts, only competing strands of subjective opinion. Relativists point to the extent to which science is a 'social construction', the product of a series of highly personal decisions by scientists about which questions to ask (and which to ignore), who to collaborate with, and which research tools to employ. Relativist critiques of science are bolstered by the difficulty of defining, in anything more than broad terms, what science actually is, and what distinguishes it from other systems of belief. Despite the best efforts of philosophers to produce a comprehensive account of the scientific method that is both flexible enough to cover all the natural sciences and detailed enough to be useful, there are still many grey areas.

Another key tenet of the relativist critique is that the 'axioms' of science are ultimately just as much faith-based assumptions as the axioms of religion or superstition. The basic principles of logic, rules about what counts as 'evidence', the belief that the universe operates according to scientific laws which we can discover through observation and experiment – these are all ideas that scientists take for granted, but that are difficult to justify except in their own terms. We know that the law of gravity has held true so far, in the bits of the universe that we can see, but what justifies our belief that it will always apply everywhere, even in the far future, and even on the other side of the universe? The belief that a contradiction can't be true seems like common sense – but it's hard to say why, other than that it would be illogical and contrary to reason. And as the sceptical 17th-century philosopher Descartes discovered when he tried to come up with some basic principles to form a firm 'foundation' for science, even the notion that the world we see before us really exists, and isn't some gigantic demonic illusion, seems impossible to prove with absolute certainty.

Leading the cultural relativist charge is the philosopher Paul Feyerabend. Feyerabend took relativism to its logical extreme, arguing that science was, in reality, just another form of mythology. Scientific ideas were merely a reflection of Western culture, no more valid or reliable than the belief systems produced by other cultures in other times and places.

Feyerabend saw modern science as a repressive ideology because of its tendency to exclude and dismiss alternative forms of explanation, such as voodoo and astrology. Just as secular democracies make a clear separation between religion and the state, Feyerabend argued that 'the separation of science and state may be our only chance to overcome the hectic barbarism of our scientific-technical age'.[28] Rather than being left in the hands of 'big-shots hiding behind a non-existing methodology', scientific ideas should be discussed democratically and put to a public vote.

Far from making their case solely through reasoned

argument, Feyerabend claimed, great scientists like Galileo had often resorted to trickery and propaganda in order to win the debate. He presented numerous other examples of scientists engaging in distortion and deception, and breaking their own rules in order to make progress. The only real method scientists followed in practice, Feyerabend insisted, was 'anything goes'.

Feyerabend's extreme cultural relativism holds obvious appeal for pseudoscientists seeking to supplant a well-supported scientific theory. By denying that the sciences have a consistent method that distinguishes them from other types of human knowledge, Feyerabend effectively abolishes the distinction between science and pseudo-science.

If science is no more valid than witchcraft or shamanism, then Aids patients really are no better off seeking help from their doctor than from a snake-oil salesman like Matthias Rath – and inexpensive 'treatments' like garlic and beetroot may be perfectly adequate substitutes for antiretroviral drugs. If one person's opinion is just as 'true' as any other's, then Peter Duesberg and David Rasnick have every right to demand that their ideas be given equal weight to those of the scientists who have actually carried out research on Aids – and Caspar Schmidt's view that Aids was nothing more than a 'mass delusion' is just as worthy of serious discussion as Robert Gallo's view that it was caused by a virus.

Feyerabend has been embraced by (among others) the

South African Aids denialist Anthony Brink, who alludes to his ideas in his lengthy treatise 'Debating AZT'.[29] Making no apologies for 'my polemical style and sardonic tone', he tells his readers that 'I wrote with politicking in mind … It's a trick I picked up from Galileo. Unable to sell his discovery of the moons of Jupiter to his peers, he took to pamphleteering to the lay public instead'.

And yet the image presented by Feyerabend is essentially a caricature. The assertion that reason is an exclusively European invention is not only historically inaccurate – it embraces many of the same inaccuracies that drove the 19th-century colonialists to believe that European culture was superior to every other. By portraying science as a product of Western culture alone, Feyerabend and other cultural relativists do a disservice to the countless non-Western thinkers through the ages who have contributed to the development of human knowledge. Gone are the Egyptian astronomers who pioneered the 365-day calendar, the Indian mathematicians who gave us the concept of 'zero', the Persians who invented algebra, the Chinese alchemists who first produced gunpowder, the medieval Arabs who pioneered the concept of 'peer review' and formulated the basic principles of the scientific method, and the herbal healers from around the globe whose remedies now form the basis of so many modern drugs. Gone too are the thousands of non-Western scientists working today – and the huge technological advances made over the last half-century in Japan and many other non-Western countries. In reality, science is – and always has been – multicultural to the core.

Feyerabend's view of science as inherently 'Western' stemmed in part from his observation that the overwhelming majority of his academic peers were (like him) white, Western, male and middle-class. But while this doubtless tells us something about the social structure of Europe and the USA in the 1970s – where the upper echelons of the media, judiciary, business and governmental sectors were all similarly white, Western and male – it's hard to see what else it really proves. Feyerabend's account of the more recent history of science is also somewhat inaccurate. While it's true that Galileo – like many modern scientists – made efforts to popularise his ideas in terms that the 'lay public' could understand, it simply isn't true that his fellow scientists refused to listen. From an early stage, Galileo was sharing his theories with the German astronomer Joseph Kepler, who confirmed Galileo's observations using his own telescope, and enthusiastically endorsed his ideas. Galileo's problem was less with his rival scientists than with the Catholic Church, which declared his theories heretical and threatened to torture and kill him. Far from supporting Feyerabend's demand that science be curtailed and controlled by the state, the case of Galileo highlights the danger of allowing a political institution to dictate what scientists can and cannot say.

Neither is it obvious that the 'socially constructed' nature of human knowledge rules out any possibility of our ideas being objective or truthful. The fact that mundane and 'unscientific' factors may influence which topic a particular researcher chooses to investigate, and who to work with in investigating it, need not prevent him or her from pursuing the investigation itself in a systematic and impartial way.

And while even the best of scientists can make mistakes, and allow their personal biases to distort their objectivity, this does not in itself prove that objectivity is a meaningless ideal. In fact, the opposite is true: it's only through comparing the reality of research practice against the theoretical ideal of objectivity that it can even make sense to talk about bias and distortion. It is impossible, for example, to highlight Clarence Cook Little's double standard over the use of animal experimentation – or the rampant charlatanism of Trofim Lysenko – without the understanding that science, as properly practised, should apply its methods in a fair and objective way.

Like those who attempt to portray mainstream scientific ideas as the product of a political conspiracy, a religious mass movement or a hysterical 'mass delusion', the pseudoscientists who characterise science as nothing more than a mythical artefact of Western culture are seeking to dismiss the evidence by shouting it down rather than by engaging with it.

While it's true that science becomes impossible without certain basic assumptions, what isn't true is that these assumptions are in any sense exclusively Western. The basic principles of logic, consistency, evidence and 'inductive reasoning' are common to every human society and present in all belief systems. The difference between science and most other forms of knowledge is that scientists try to restrict the assumptions they make to these essential, core principles. The fact that absolute, irreducible certainty is beyond our reach may well give us good reason to treat all scientific theories as provisional and subject to revision. But this is no justification for rejecting the strongest explanation currently available in favour of wishful thinking. Our beliefs may all be fallible, but this does not mean that they are all equally valid.

Pseudoscience and peer review

Modern science is so specialised that there is simply no way that any one person can become competent in every area. Faced with two competing theories about smoking and cancer, or Aids and HIV, or asbestos, or Marxist-Leninist agro-biology, few of us will have any means of being sure, just by reading the text in front of us, which is good science and which is bogus. From debates about public health to controversies over the environment, we will often have little choice but to trust one expert opinion or another.

Pseudoscientists exploit this gap between expert knowledge and public opinion. As time passes and science becomes ever more complex, this gap is only going to get bigger. Yet at the same time, it is now far easier to check up on the background of those presented to us as 'experts' – and the track record of the journalists doing the presenting – than it would have been even ten or fifteen years ago.

In order to be published in journals such as *Nature* or *The Lancet*, research papers have to be checked and approved by an anonymous panel of independent experts in the area under investigation. While there have been some high-profile cases where flawed or fraudulent research has been published even after such scrutiny, the peer review process does at least add an additional layer of protection. In general, a theory presented in a peer-reviewed scientific journal will have been more rigorously examined than one that has only ever appeared in a column in the *Sunday Telegraph*.

The more difficult cases are those where pseudoscience is being peddled by someone with a credible scientific track record. Speaking to the *New York Times* in 2007, the UK's Astronomer Royal, Martin Rees, bemoaned a tendency among some of his ageing peers – as the newspaper put it – 'to strike off half-cocked into unfamiliar territory' towards the tail end of their career.[30] Unlike composers, Rees argued, 'there are few scientists whose last works are their greatest'. Examples listed by the *New York Times* include the leading Aids denialist Peter Duesberg, and the Nobel prize-winner Kary Mullis who, alongside Aids denial,[31] has advocated astrology and expounded the virtues of LSD.

A reputable scientist may also lose his objectivity in his efforts to discredit a new theory that threatens to eclipse the area that he has spent his life researching. This – along with the fact that he had been co-opted by the tobacco industry – may help to explain the staunch opposition of the cancer geneticist Clarence Cook Little to any suggestion that lung cancer could be caused by an environmental factor such as smoking.

Or it may be that a scientist with expertise in one area, such as biology, falls flat on his face in attempting a critique of another, such as epidemiology. Towards the end of the 19th century, the proponent of evolution Alfred Russel Wallace conducted a long campaign to convince the world that smallpox vaccinations were a 'delusion' with 'injurious effects', and that they were being promoted by 'interested parties' within the medical profession.[32] As with Aids denialism, many of Wallace's objections focused on the gaps that then existed in germ theory. While there was overwhelming statistical evidence that vaccination could significantly reduce the incidence of smallpox, until the early 20th century there was far less understanding of how, exactly, it worked. Wallace, in turn, was accused by the medical journal *The Lancet* of being highly selective in his choice of data, and of simply ignoring large amounts of statistical evidence that were inconsistent with his views.

Just as a trusted newspaper or TV channel can occasionally get things catastrophically wrong, so too can a scientist with a well-respected track record. For the lay person, the solution, as with the media, is to check as wide a range of sources as possible, and to try to get a sense of the broad consensus among scientists. Many scientific journals now publish research reports online, so it's much easier to compare what the scientists themselves are saying with how their views have been reported. If an established scientific theory is being questioned, does the argument focus on the evidence? Or does it rely on a conspiracy theory, an appeal to relativism, a political ideology, a religious assertion or unsubstantiated claims about 'mass hysteria'? If the views of a particular scientist seem dubious, what do his or her peers have to say on the issue? Are there any clear cases of this scientist distorting data, ignoring good evidence or applying double standards in evaluating evidence? Or are the criticisms less about their methods and more about their politics or alleged motivations? Are those being characterised as 'sceptics' pursuing a genuinely balanced and objective approach, or are they dismissing valid evidence on unreasonable grounds? If the issue is being presented as 'controversial', is that controversy genuine or manufactured?

Scientific consensus is not, of course, infallible. There have been many cases where the consensus has initially rejected a new theory until very strong evidence has been accumulated to support it. And given that science proceeds on the basis of evidence, the consensus of scientific opinion tends naturally to favour established ideas over new and untested ones. But there are far fewer examples of the scientific consensus converging around a positive claim – such as the claim that cigarettes cause cancer – only for this subsequently to be shown to be false.

It is not strictly impossible that the editors of every peer-reviewed journal in the world could jointly conspire to silence and exclude a genuine expert. But in practice, given the number of such journals, this would take an enormous amount of effort and co-ordination. Without compelling evidence of such a conspiracy, it seems reasonable to assume that someone who has failed to publish any research in any such journal is probably not a genuine scientific expert.

CHAPTER TWELVE

THE EMPEROR'S NEW PARADIGM

Training yourself to think unthinkable thoughts has
advantages beyond the thoughts themselves ... If you
can think things so outside the box that they'd make
people's hair stand on end, you'll have no trouble with
the small trips outside the box that people call inno-
vative.

Paul Graham, 'What You Can't Say'[1]

Businesses thrive by finding new opportunities to make
money, or inventing new ways of doing old things more
cheaply. In a booming market, where the biggest fear of
business is that the competition may cash in on the 'next
big thing' before you do, a clever new concept – be it a
social networking website or a new way of selling mort-
gages – can be sold off for millions of dollars, even when
it's far from clear that the idea is sustainable in the long
term.

The result has been a culture where creative thinking
has acquired a near-mystical status, and where the gap
between rhetoric and reality can often seem perilously
thin. Some organisations will pay enormous sums of

money to those promising to help them 'think outside the box', 'challenge the orthodoxy', 'push the envelope', 'take a blue sky approach', 'drive through change' or bring about a 'paradigm shift'.

It may seem ironic that the growth of an industry dedicated to teaching people how to think in innovative ways should have led to such a massive over-production of pre-fabricated clichés, but in some ways it makes perfect sense. In a market where concepts have become a commodity, it's possible to make money not only from brilliant new ideas, but also from mediocre ideas cleverly packaged in brilliant-sounding rhetoric.

In the dot-com boom of the late 1990s, investors were persuaded to put millions of dollars into new technology companies, often with no idea of how those companies were going to make money, other than that they would be doing it via the internet. The net was a 'new paradigm', explained the experts, where the old rules of business simply did not apply. It was time for new rules. It was time, announced the *Financial Times* in February 2000, to 'throw the rule-book out of the window'.[2]

'Traditional management techniques are just not flexible or fast enough for e-environments, nor do they recognise the different sorts of people and cultures involved,' one management consultant told the newspaper. Others reported that established companies were still too 'risk-averse', and 'slowed down by old-style thinking'. Yet another complained that there was an 'intolerance of failure' in the UK and the rest of Europe. 'If you've been bankrupt in the US, it shows you're willing to be entrepreneurial and take risks. Over here, if you're bankrupt, it's still seen as evidence of moral turpitude.'

The following month the NASDAQ technology stock market peaked, and soon began to slide. In May 2000, the online clothing retailer Boo.com – which the *Financial Times* had described as a company 'in the pan-European vanguard' – went into insolvency, having lost a reported $120 million in six months. A rush of others soon followed. By October 2002 the NASDAQ had plummeted, and investors were a gob-smacking $5 trillion poorer.

But if there was a Nobel Prize for 'Unthinkable thinking', the senior management of the Enron Corporation would surely be among the top contenders. Enron's first unthinkable idea was to bring the rigours of the free market to the tired old over-regulated US energy industry. Instead of just generating and supplying gas or electricity, Enron began trading energy 'derivatives' – contractual agreements to buy or sell a specific amount of gas, oil or electricity for a particular price on a particular day. This proved attractive to companies who wanted to protect themselves from sudden fluctuations in price. And it created a new financial product that could be bought or sold for a profit, just like stocks and shares. Enron became very good at doing just that, and used the resulting cash to expand rapidly, taking over more and more of its rivals and using its growing power to lobby for more deregulation.

Enron's second unthinkable idea was to move beyond energy and into other markets. The company began buying and selling 'derivatives' in everything from TV advertising to insurance and high-speed data transmission. Some of these schemes worked, but others didn't – and the firm began to make serious losses. To get around this problem, Enron came up with its most unthinkable idea of all. The company would use its convoluted financial structure to hide its losses and give the impression that it was far more profitable than it actually was, thus keeping its share price artificially high.

Enron executives played clever accounting tricks to make bad debts look like profits and make real profits seem hyper-real, all the while telling themselves that as long as the share price kept going up, everything would be OK. For many, the fact that it was so unclear just *how* Enron was managing to make such massive profits simply added to the mystique. Clearly this was a bunch of rule-book-busting blue-sky thinkers living in a new paradigm that the rest of us, encumbered by our 'old-style thinking', just didn't get.

For a business with the slogan 'Ask Why', Enron was surprisingly coy about financial questions. The company refused, for 'competitive reasons', to reveal key details about its operations – while insisting that those who described it as a 'black box' were either ignorant or mean, or both. 'People who raise questions are people who have not gone through [our business] in detail and who want to throw rocks at us', insisted Enron CEO Jeffrey Skilling when, in March 2001, Bethany McLean of *Fortune* magazine first began to do just that.[3]

Fortune had named Enron as 'America's Most Innovative Company' for six consecutive years. Now it was the first to ask publicly whether the company might have been overvalued. Within months, the company's share price was sliding. In August 2001, CEO Jeffrey Skilling resigned from the company, citing 'personal' reasons – after having cashed in an estimated $33 million in Enron stock.[4] As criticisms began to grow, Enron's chairman Kenneth Lay accused one New York columnist of launching an 'attack' on Enron in order to 'discredit the free-market system'.[5] But by November the company was admitting that it had massively overstated its earnings. Enron's share price was now just 61 cents – less than 1 per cent of what it had been twelve months earlier. On 2 December, the company filed for bankruptcy with debts of roughly $23 billion. It was, at the time, the biggest corporate collapse in US history.

Bubbles and booms

Enron got away with lying about its profits for so long by creating a financial structure that sounded very clever, but was understood by almost nobody. When the company was forced to explain how it operated, it did so in language that seems, with the benefit of hindsight, to have been calculated to confuse. Enron's business, the company claimed, involved 'derivative instruments which eliminated the contingent nature of existing restricted forward contracts'. These enabled it 'to hedge certain merchant investments and other assets'.[6]

'A big part of what drives market bubbles is delusion', commented the *Wall Street Journal* a few months after Enron's collapse.[7] 'We are so convinced that some revolutionary shift is rewriting the laws of supply and demand – whether for tulips or telecommunications – we don't care what the words in the storytelling actually mean. The less we understand, the more we buy in.' Enron had 'relied on a dictionary's worth of confusing terms to sell a story people wanted to believe'.

Despite all the effort that Enron had put into making itself look new and shiny, the essence of the scam was really just a new variation of a very old trick. Like the victims of a mock auction, handing over their cash to a cockney with a megaphone in exchange for a sealed box full of junk, thousands of ordinary people had been persuaded to sink their savings into Enron with no real idea of what they were getting into. They'd been sold a pig in a poke – suppressing any doubts with the continual reassurance that this was a 'new paradigm' where the old rules of economics were obsolete.

The word 'paradigm' has an unusual history. For several hundred years it was mainly confined to the abstract world of linguistics, where it was used to refer to a particular sort of grammatical pattern – e.g. 'I eat', 'you eat', 'he eats', 'she eats', 'we eat', 'they eat'.[8] But in 1962, an American philosopher called Thomas Kuhn wrote a book called *The Structure of Scientific Revolutions,* which – despite its dry-sounding name – eventually became one of the most successful academic texts ever written. Kuhn used the word 'paradigm' to refer to an established set of theoretical rules within science, such as Newtonian physics or Einstein's theory of relativity.

Where previous thinkers had tended to see natural science as a steady process of evolution, with each new theory building on the last, Kuhn believed that it was more like a series of revolutions. When Einstein had supplanted the Newtonian 'paradigm', Kuhn argued, he hadn't just tweaked Newton's rules – he'd thrown them out completely. Faced with a growing number of problems in physics that Newton's theories simply couldn't deal with, Einstein had come up with an entirely new set of rules, based on a radically different set of assumptions. Yet even when these rules had been shown to work much better than Newton's, a stubborn old guard within the scientific community refused to acknowledge the new reality, and continued to cling to the old and obsolete paradigm. In the words of Max Planck, Kuhn suggested that 'a new scientific truth does not triumph by convincing its opponents ... but rather because its opponents eventually die, and a new generation grows up that is familiar with it.'

Philosophers remain divided over how realistic this description of the scientific process actually is. But regardless of its accuracy as a theory, as a cultural myth it has been hugely influential. At its most vulgar, the legend of the new paradigm is a classic story of good guys versus bad guys. The young, genius visionary has a radical new idea that's going to transform the world – but the stale old fogies just don't get it. They are so bogged down in their old ways of thinking that they are incapable of understanding why the new paradigm is so great. He is Galileo, Georges Danton, Bob Dylan, Jesus Christ, Albert Einstein, Charles Darwin and Richard Branson. They are the Pope, Louis XVI, the Pharisees, those other scientists, British Airways and Richard Nixon. He is the Proto-Mammal, destined to take over the planet. They are the dinosaurs, earmarked for extinction. He is Captain Kirk, boldly going where no man has gone before. He is Evel Knievel, Elvis and Batman. They don't understand that they must innovate or die. They don't understand that the kids just wanna rock.

The rhetoric of the 'new paradigm' works so well as propaganda because it sounds like a neutral, scientific term when in practice it's thoroughly political. As soon as we agree that a particular idea or business method is a new paradigm, the argument is over. The new paradigm is a good thing by definition – not only good, in fact, but inevitable, and anyone stupid enough to resist it is obsolete, laughable and doomed.

Yet it seems questionable whether the concept of a 'paradigm shift' really adds anything useful to discussions about life outside the laboratory. This isn't to say that nothing ever changes, or that it isn't often necessary to re-evaluate our assumptions and rules. But it's difficult to find a social or economic change in the last 4,000 years that has required the kind of wholesale conceptual demolition involved, for example, in Einstein's realisation that time slows down the faster you move, that space is curved (and expanding), and that trees, people and sunlight are ultimately all made out of the same stuff. The danger of 'new paradigm' rhetoric is that it asks us to suspend our rational judgement and engage in an act of faith. The call to 'throw the rule book out of the window' is too often a thinly veiled demand that we disregard the lessons of the past and trust in the inherent brilliantness of a phenomenon that, due to its revolutionary new nature, cannot yet be fully understood.

The dream of the unfettered free market, where government never interferes and the only rule is that there are no rules, may be appealing, but it's also delusional. Every trade is underwritten by the assurance that the sellers will be held accountable in the courts if they act dishonestly. If we take that protection away, then investors will simply stop investing and the market will collapse. Had every company been behaving like Enron, there wouldn't have been a market to defraud in the first place.

At the time of writing, roughly 170 news articles containing the phrase 'paradigm shift' or 'new paradigm' were being published on the internet every week. The laws of economics may be more malleable than the laws of human nature – and given the events of recent years it seems plausible that a Copernican rethink is overdue. But so long as we have an economy based around one lot of people making things that other people want to buy, we should, in the words of the Bank of England governor Mervyn King, 'be cautious … Paradigm is a word too often used by those who would like to have a new idea but cannot think of one'.[9]

CHAPTER THIRTEEN

THE GOD DILUTION

First the Buddhist talked of the ways to calm, the mastery of desire, the path of enlightenment, and the panellists all said 'Wow, terrific, if that works for you that's great.' Then the Hindu talked of the cycles of suffering and birth and rebirth, the teachings of Krishna and the way to release, and they all said 'Wow, terrific, if that works for you that's great.' And so on, until the Catholic priest talked of the message of Jesus Christ, the promise of salvation and the way to life eternal, and they all said 'Wow, terrific, if that works for you that's great.' And he thumped the table and shouted: 'No! It's not a question of it if works for me! It's the true word of the living God, and if you don't believe it you're all damned to Hell!' And they all said: 'Wow, terrific, if that works for you that's great.'

Simon Blackburn, 'Does Relativism Matter?'[1]

In the UK's 2001 national census, 390,000 people identified their religious affiliation as 'Jedi' – a figure which easily surpassed the reported numbers of Buddhists, Jews and Sikhs.[2] In the Australian census of the same year, more than 70,000 Jedi came out of the woodwork, light-sabres-a-waving,[3] while in New Zealand 1.5 per cent of the population declared their allegiance, making 'Jediism' the second-largest recorded religion in the country. The majority of self-declared Jedi seem to have joined in either as a joke or as a protest against organised religion. But there are some followers who seem deadly serious, notwith-standing the fact that their faith began life as a fictional creed in a sci-fi trilogy.

'We all walk our own path in Jediism', explains the website www.jediismway.org,[4] outlining some basic tenets of the faith. Jedi believe that 'the guidance of the Force will bring us to a course of right action. As a result, some have been guided to a belief in a God and others have not, but all believe that the Force will set them on their best path possible'. The Force is 'that so called "Mystical", "Holy", or "Unexplainable" energy found in nearly every religion and science philosophy … this energy guides, invigorates or is generated by life, it may be used or tapped into with proper training, and is infinite in its potential'. And while Jediism may not be for everyone, it seems tempting to conclude that if that's what works for them, that's great.

Karl Marx famously described religion as the 'opium of the people', an analogy which may sound more dismis-sive today than was originally intended. In the 19th century, opium was legal across Europe, and a widely used painkiller. Marx's point was that if we could remove the injustice that was giving the proletarian masses such a headache, then the desire for the consolations of religion would also begin to fade.

A century and a half later, it looks as though Marx may have been partly right. As inequality and deprivation have fallen across the industrialised world, so too has the prevalence of religious belief. And yet even where religion has declined most, in countries such as the UK, it nonetheless remains a significant force. While Britons have deserted the churches in their droves, two-thirds still profess to a belief either in a God or in some other form of 'higher power', Jediist or otherwise.

For many people in formerly devoutly Christian countries, the vacuum left by the decline of organised religion has been filled not by atheism, but by a vague, slimmed-down, 'mysticism-lite' that affords many of the comforts of traditional faith without any of the usual baggage. You can still have the afterlife, a rough sense of purpose, and the vague feeling that doing the right thing will bring some reward. But you don't have to follow a prescriptive set of rules, or stand in a cold building every Sunday listening to dreary sermons. And you get to play with lightsabres.

The desire to numb the pain of economic hardship may be one reason for religious belief, but it seems unlikely to be the only one. Even if human injustice could be eliminated completely, we would still have to endure the horror of accidents and natural disasters, the pain of illness and ageing, the grief of losing those we love, and the fear of our own mortality. And many of us would still struggle from time to time with the nagging feeling that our lives lacked meaning or direction.

Religious belief provides a reassuring answer to all of these things: however painful, lonely or unfair life may seem, in the end, and in ways that surpass human understanding, everything will turn out OK. Good deeds will be rewarded, suffering atoned for, death shall lose its sting, and the Force will be with you.

More than this, religion offers a framework for living – a 'design for life' that has evolved over generations. For millions around the world, faith is as much a matter of cultural identity as a personal choice, bringing a sense of connection to traditions and customs stretching back thousands of years.

Religion is, in a sense, the ultimate pig in a poke. While adherents may look for rational proof to support the belief in an all-powerful, all-knowing, benevolent creator God, it's a view that is based not on evidence, but on faith. And for many monotheists this is precisely the point: taking God at his word, without demanding absolute proof, is an expression of trust and loyalty, and an important spiritual duty. As Jesus tells the doubting St Thomas, 'Blessed are those who have not seen and yet believe'. But the problem – with religion as with all areas of life – is that those 'who have not seen, and yet believe' can leave themselves open to exploitation. If religious faith is the opium of people, then it's clear that the side effects can sometimes be disastrous.

Fundamentalism

Alongside a belief in God, many strands of Christianity, Islam and to a lesser extent Judaism have traditionally required believers to accept, on faith, the absolute truth of a prescribed list of written beliefs, and to adhere to a set of inflexible rules. This literal-mindedness seems peculiar to the monotheistic religions. Hinduism, Buddhism and Taoism tend, by contrast, to downplay the extent to which religious truth can be contained in written form, and to emphasise personal experience and intuition over rigid adherence to scripture. And whereas within the Eastern religions, a wide spectrum of beliefs have traditionally been permitted – from polytheism to atheism – Islam, Judaism and Christianity have drawn clear lines between accepted beliefs and heresy.

Within modern Christianity, the insistence on the literal truth of the Bible has been strongest within Protestantism, which began as a reaction against the corruption of Christian teachings by the Catholic Church. During the Middle Ages, the Catholic clergy played a central role in interpreting the Bible on behalf of ordinary people. At a time when the overwhelming majority of the population was illiterate and uneducated, this created enormous potential for abuse.

In any system predicated on absolute truth being

overseen and interpreted by a priestly class, inspired as much by mystical revelation as by reason and logic, there is a clear risk that the priests might be tempted to twist things for their own ends – or those of their commercial sponsors. In medieval Europe, the Catholic Church acquired immense wealth by telling rich people that they could buy their way into Heaven by paying monks to pray for them, emphatically endorsed the notion that kings and queens had a divinely ordained right to rule their subjects, and publicly sanctioned the persecution of Jews. Given these and other abuses, it is perhaps understandable that many Christians would feel driven to insist that the truths of the Bible are fixed, and not open to adjustment or reinterpretation. But while this may reduce the risk of corruption by priestly middle-men, it creates many other problems.

Throughout the ages, most systems of knowledge – from medicine to agriculture to engineering – have been flexible enough to allow for revision when better ideas came along. But if a holy book is taken to be the absolute and infallible word of an all-knowing, all-powerful God, then this seems to exclude the possibility of anyone ever refining or improving upon it. An infallible God would, presumably, never need to do a second draft.

While Hindus and Buddhists, not being bound to a set of dictats about the nature of the physical world, have relatively little to fear from science, the theories of modern biology and physics pose a mortal threat to the beliefs of many Christian fundamentalists. Those who are committed to the literal truth of the Bible are forced into defending a creation story written several thousand years ago, and have little choice but to reject the theory of evolution, along with most of modern physics.

Worse still, all of the original manuscripts of the Bible have been lost. So if we want to hang on to the absolute truth of the modern Bible, on top of believing in the infallibility of the original texts we must also believe that the surviving copies are accurate reproductions. And unless we are fluent in Hebrew, Aramaic and Ancient Greek, we need to believe that the available translations of those copies faithfully reflect their intended meaning. In short, in order to have faith in the literal truth of today's Bible, we need to believe in the infallibility not only of the original writers of the Biblical texts, but also all of the editors, copyists and translators who have worked to produce the version that we read today.

In practice, belief in the literal truth of the Bible often leads to exactly the kinds of problems that it was supposed to help us avoid. Because the book seems oblique and counter-intuitive in so many places, it is sometimes very difficult to establish what the correct literal interpretation of any given passage should actually be. At that point we must either simply give up, or seek help from a modern-day preacher who may have an agenda of his or her own.

A further problem is that the Bible contains many

teachings that seem to contradict each other. Some parts of the text, for example, appear to support the persecution of homosexuals, while others advocate universal love and compassion. Alongside these, there are some apparent factual contradictions – even between accounts of the life of Jesus written by his surviving disciples. If the Bible is the highest form of truth available, then it's hard to see how we could have any objective framework for choosing between two apparently contradictory teachings.

Believers might respond by asserting that the holy book's contradictions only seem that way because all human understanding is limited and flawed. Or they might take a different tack and assert that in matters of religion, and for reasons beyond our understanding, two contradictory statements can both simultaneously be true.

At its extreme, fundamentalism can lead believers to suspend even the most basic principles of logic and evidence in an effort to hang on to the infallibility of a particular set of written doctrines. And perhaps this is one reason why fundamentalism has so often led to violence. Once we dispense with reason, discussion becomes impossible, and the only method of persuasion left is brute force.

Faith within reason

The disillusionment felt by many today towards mainstream Christianity reflects a wider hostility towards all forms of organised religion in a number of formerly devout countries. From sectarian killings in Northern Ireland to the death cult of suicide bombing, once you start listing examples from recent history of bad things that have been done in the name of one religion or another, it's difficult to stop. The biologist Richard Dawkins has done this with aplomb in recent years, spurred on by horror over the September 11th attacks and the rise of fundamentalism, both Christian and Islamic.

To Dawkins, it seems obvious that there is no good reason to believe that our lives have any cosmic purpose beyond the goals and objectives that we set for ourselves, that this life will continue in any meaningful form after our bodies have died, or that there is a creator God watching over us who cares about such matters.

Not only is religious belief harmful, Dawkins argues, it is also childish. 'There is something infantile,' he suggests, 'in the presumption that somebody else (parents in the case of children, God in the case of adults) has a responsibility to give your life meaning.'[5] It is inherently more noble and mature, Dawkins suggests, to find one's own meaning in life and face the 'strong keen wind of understanding'[6] without the false comforts of religion.

Dawkins believes that even seemingly moderate forms of religion can have harmful consequences. By creating a climate in which people are encouraged to believe things that can't be justified on the basis of evidence, he argues, religion devalues critical thought, leaving our society vulnerable to exploitation by those seeking to disseminate dangerous untruths. Faith is an evil, Dawkins argues, 'precisely because it requires no justification and brooks no argument ... Teaching children that unquestioned faith is a virtue primes them ... to grow up into potentially lethal weapons for future jihads or crusades'.[7]

It's easy to agree with Dawkins that the promotion of unquestioned faith is both reckless and potentially disastrous. But where his position seems weakest is in his apparent assumption that all faith is necessarily 'unquestioned faith' which 'brooks no argument'. To define faith as the stubborn defence of an arbitrary belief, even in the face of overwhelming evidence that the belief is false, is to accept the fundamentalists' definition from the outset. This paints out of the picture generations of thinkers who have approached their religious belief not as a dogmatic certainty, but as an ongoing struggle, subject to the constraints of reason and doubt.

Neither do you have to be religious to be a fundamentalist. Alongside the crimes that have been committed on the basis of unquestioned faith in religion, the last 100 years have seen a succession of disasters committed in the name of some dogmatic secular 'faith' or another. Nazi ideology was based on an absolute belief in the ideas of Adolf Hitler, and the racial superduperness of the German people. Unquestioned faith in the wisdom of Marxist-Leninist revolutionary theory led to disaster in the Soviet Union. And when scientists seek to place their work beyond question, as did Stalin's 'barefoot scientist' Trofim Lysenko, the results can also be catastrophic.

Religion as 'regulated wishful thinking'

There is a meaningful distinction between believing something in the face of strong evidence that the belief is false, and believing something in the absence of concrete evidence one way or the other. For example, most of us – regardless of our beliefs about what happens *after* our lives have ended – tend to assume that there are plenty of good things still in store for us, and that we will, at least, live out our natural lifespan. It suits us to take an optimistic approach to life, even though we have no rational way of knowing what the future holds. And there is some evidence that this sort of irrational faith in the future is actually good for us, making us happier and healthier, and improving our chances of success in life.

But it's possible to be an optimist about the future without being dogmatic about it. I hope and believe – though I have no way of being sure – that I will live to see my 80th birthday. It's a useful belief, in the sense that people who expect to live a long and happy life tend to increase their chances of doing so. But it's a belief that is nonetheless subject to reasoned revision. If I were to find out next week that I was suffering from a terminal disease, I would have to start rethinking my faith pretty quickly. It would only be if, like the Aids denialists, I failed to accept the evidence of my illness that I would be crossing the line from faith into dogma.

As we saw in chapter 1, people tend to delude themselves least about questions for which there is clear, objective evidence. While most people see themselves as above average in terms of vague qualities such as 'warmth' and 'friendliness', they tend to have a much more realistic view of more quantifiable traits like intelligence. The point about a belief in the existence of something beyond the confines of the material world – such as a belief in God or an afterlife – is that it is a belief which, by definition, cannot be proved or disproved by evidence.

The evidence from psychology seems to suggest that most of us rely on one fantasy or another – 'infantile' or otherwise – in order to remain happy. From the irrational self-belief that makes us think we are cleverer, more beautiful, more talented or more popular than we really are, to the irrational optimism that leads us to believe in an unrealistically rosy future, most of us, religious or not, seem to need to kid ourselves about many things, much of the time.

And maybe this shouldn't be too much of a surprise. If human beings are just the random product of mindless evolutionary forces, and if our capacity for intelligence developed primarily because it made us more effective hunters, why should we expect that we could all function happily while living face-to-face with the full facts of our existence – that our basic psychological needs would always match up neatly with the truths of subatomic physics?

It's not only traditional religious ideas like God and the afterlife that tend to wither and disintegrate when exposed to 'the strong keen wind of understanding'. Once we take the immortal soul out of the equation, even the idea of ourselves as individual beings whose existence endures steadily throughout one lifetime seems difficult to sustain: along with most of the rest of our body, the cells in our brain are regularly dying off and being replaced, and over a seven-year time period the whole brain is regenerated. Odd though it may seem, the person writing these words now is made out of almost entirely different physical matter than the 'me' of early 2001. And that 'me' was a different lump of molecules again from the person who started university in 1994. Many philosophers have tried to explain how, given that no material within our bodies seems to endure through our whole lifetime, we can still be said to be the same person, rather than a continuous series of self-replicating clones. To me at least, these efforts seem reminiscent of the Catholic Church's quixotic attempt to give a rational justification for its position on homosexuality. If the brain thinking these thoughts now will have been entirely destroyed and replaced with an imperfect copy within the next seven years, then it's difficult to see any rational reason for believing that it could genuinely be the same 'me' that will read these words in 2016. From this point of view, it's not only life after death, but life after the next decade that is looking doubtful. If I am lucky enough to make it to my 80th birthday, the 'me' that sits there blowing out the candles will be several incarnations removed from the one sitting here now.

Likewise, if the human mind is essentially the same thing as the human brain, and if the brain is no more than a cleverly arranged collection of atoms and molecules knocking together in interesting ways, then the notion of free will also starts to seem decidedly shaky. If our thoughts are nothing but a complex causal chain of chemical signals and electrical impulses, then we are surely little more than organic robots. Sophisticated robots, no doubt, following a highly complex set of continually evolving programs and procedures – but robots nonetheless, different from our digital watches only by a matter of degree.

This, for me, is the limit of scepticism. I can see no rational solution to these doubts, and yet in order to live a normal life I have to hide them well away from the 'strong keen wind of understanding', otherwise things just start seeming too weird. As we saw earlier in the book, even the idea that the material world that we think we see before us is *real* – that we aren't all the victim of some strange all-encompassing illusion – is ultimately something that cannot be proven through reasoned argument alone. There comes a point, it seems, at which all of us have to embrace some faith-based belief or another, otherwise normal life simply becomes impossible.

For those of us who feel loved and liked, who find their everyday lives fulfilling and who believe that they have some reason to count themselves lucky, this need is doubtless reduced; 'facing straight into the strong keen wind of understanding' may well be an easy choice, and faith-based assumptions can be kept to a bare minimum. But for those who feel lonely or insecure, for those grieving the death of a loved one, for those stuck in dead-end jobs, for those who feel that their lives lack purpose or significance or who simply feel a need for meaning that transcends everyday life, it seems easy to see why reason alone could feel hopelessly inadequate, and why some form of religion might be appealing and useful.

One way of thinking about religious faith is that it is a decision to take on, in the apparent absence of compelling evidence either for or against, a set of beliefs that cheer some people up, give them a sense of identity and purpose and help them get to sleep at night. Religion – at least on one level – is wishful thinking, strategically deployed.

This comment, from a contributor to a debate on the website of the *Guardian* newspaper, seems fairly typical:

> Becoming a Muslim has made me much more contented than I have ever been previously in my

life. So, in that way, even if it were all untrue and after death I would turn to dust, then I wouldn't have lost out … In fact, my short life would have been enriched no end by the joy I have experienced in prayer, on pilgrimage, or with my brothers and sisters in faith.[8]

Radical atheists may dismiss this kind of reasoning as 'infantile', but in some ways it seems quite pragmatic: if, from an objective standpoint, our existence *is* ultimately meaningless, then it's hard to see why it should matter if some people choose to believe, without evidence, in a comforting and harmless delusion.

Harmless delusions tend to be vague, untestable or both. Thus a soldier's fuzzy faith in having been 'born lucky' seems relatively unproblematic, and may even be beneficial if it leads him to fight with more determination. A belief that he is physically invulnerable to bullets, on the other hand, is liable to have catastrophic consequences. Likewise, a belief that there is a benevolent God 'somewhere up there' who cares about our lives, and wants us to be nice to people, seems frankly quite benign. But the further conviction that this God is a man, and that his views about how we should live have been recorded in detail in a particular religious text, overseen by an ageing archbishop living in a palace in Rome whose orders we are duty bound to follow, again seems much more dangerous.

If religion is the opium of the people, then most recreational users I know seem to manage their habit fairly comfortably. I suspect this may be because the wiser strands of religious tradition are quite upfront about their limitations. The knowledge that the creed can never be proved rationally, beyond reasonable doubt, can give adherents a certain degree of intellectual humility. It seems to me that the difficulty is less with religion itself than with the *politicisation* of religion – the gifting of worldly authority to some person who is deemed to be the custodian of absolute truth. It's not so much faith in God that is the problem – it's faith in human beings.

CHAPTER FOURTEEN

HEROES AND VILLAINS

It used to be fashionable to say that there was no such thing as human nature. There was a debate over whether our behaviour was governed by 'nature' or 'nurture', and which side you took tended to depend on where you stood politically. If you were a certain kind of socialist, then you were committed to believing it was nurture all the way – that under a fair and just political system the evils of greed, corruption, war, racism, crime and religion would disappear, and we would all live happily together, farm tools and machine guns in hand, smiling down from a big red propaganda poster.

This view is less popular nowadays largely because, from Maoist China to Pol Pot's Cambodia, every attempt to reshape human nature through massive social re-engineering has had disastrous results. Tens of millions of deaths later, it seems that Trofim Lysenko's comrades were wrong after all, and that the human capacities for sadism, selfishness, bigotry, blind faith and self-delusion are not merely a product of the evil capitalist system.

Yet despite the evidence of history, the belief in the non-existence of human nature still lives on in milder guises. One of these is the conviction that human nature operates differently for 'us' (i.e. the West) than for everyone else. This might be because our civilisation has finally reached the 'End of History', rampaging across the finish line with the triumph of Western capitalism while other, more backward cultures still struggle along through the dark ages. Or it may be because our religion is the one true faith, pure and incorruptible, which allows us to transcend human folly, live as God intended and understand things as they truly are. Or it could even be because we are the sceptics who can see through all that nonsense, dispelling every superstition with the firm glare of reason and taking Occam's razor to the vines and tendrils of mumbo-jumbo. But either way, it's easy to assume that there is something about our culture, sub-culture or ideology that makes us fundamentally different from all those other chumps, with their Führers, voodoo dolls and decadent cultural values.

As we saw in chapter 1, the conviction that we are an exception to the rules of human nature is itself a common feature of human nature. Likewise, the belief in the 'exceptionalism' of one's own culture has been held by many throughout history – from the Romans who thought the gods had given them a divine right to rule Europe, to the crusaders of medieval Christianity and the missionaries of the colonial era who were convinced that their culture was uniquely 'civilised'.

During the 18th and 19th centuries, European colonists set about imposing 'civilisation' from the Congo to the

Indian subcontinent, sweeping away long-standing traditions and social structures in the process. Notwithstanding the cynicism that drove colonialism at the political level, it shouldn't be forgotten that many of those doing the colonising genuinely thought that they were bringing great benefits by sharing – albeit by force – a system of values they believed to be far superior to anything that the locals had to offer. Even now, many Westerners still struggle to understand the enormous gap between the high-minded ideals of colonialism, and the grim reality of the corruption and abuse that it produced. As we saw earlier in the case of Aids denialism, according to some sections of the political left, the lesson of colonialism – along with fascism, communism, globalisation and now the global 'war on terror' – has been that, far from being uniquely enlightened, Western culture is uniquely cruel, violent and inhumane.

It's an attractive idea, in some ways, because it allows us to hope that by reforming our culture we can ensure that the mistakes of the past are never repeated. And by blaming everything on nurture rather than nature, we can continue to believe that the sadism of the Nazis, the atrocities of Stalin, the fanaticism of Islamic extremism and the delusions that led to the Iraq war were accidents of history, caused by something 'out there' – rather than a reflection of innate human tendencies that we ourselves share. Yet the evidence suggests that, regardless of our cultural background, many of us will blithely electrocute another human being if a man in a white coat tells us to, or commit gross acts of torture and humiliation if we think we can get away with it. We can try to build societies where slavish obedience to authority is discouraged, where virtue is rewarded, where the opportunity to do horrible things is reduced, and where our need for fantasy and self-delusion can find safe outlets. But we can never kill these instincts completely.

The danger in denying our own capacity for sadism is that we become blind to it, and thereby less able to keep it in check. And by convincing ourselves that opponents or outsiders are inherently evil people, with a fundamentally different nature from our own, we kill our capacity for compassion and it becomes far easier to let our sadistic impulses run riot.

Throwing the rule-book out with the bathwater

I remember that my first response to the reports of abuse and torture at Guantánamo Bay was to accuse the accusers of exaggeration or deliberate deception. I didn't believe America would ever do those things ... It struck me as a no-brainer that this stuff was being invented by the far left or was part of Al Qaeda propaganda. After all, they train captives to lie about this stuff, don't they? Bottom line: I trusted the president in a time of war to obey the rule of law that we were and are defending.

Andrew Sullivan, *The Times*[1]

In an order signed just a few months after the September 2001 terror attacks in New York, US president George W. Bush announced that 'the war against terrorism ushers in a new paradigm' which 'requires new thinking in the law of war'.[2] Al Qaeda terrorists and their Afghan Taleban allies were 'unlawful combatants' to whom the terms of the Geneva Conventions simply didn't apply. US forces in Afghanistan would 'continue to treat detainees humanely' and broadly in line with 'the principles of Geneva', but only where this was 'consistent with military necessity'.

White House lawyers argued that the law on torture only prohibited interrogation methods that caused 'pain equivalent in intensity to the pain accompanying serious physical injury, such as organ failure, impairment of bodily function, or even death', or 'significant psychological harm of significant duration, e.g., lasting for months or even years'.[3] Any form of coercion that fell short of this could be permitted, if 'military necessity' seemed to require it.

The American government authorised a series of painful 'enhanced interrogation techniques' for use in extracting information from terror suspects detained at the Guantánamo Bay military base in Cuba. These included prolonged exposure to loud music and bright lights, intimidation with dogs, forced nudity, and compelling prisoners to adopt uncomfortable 'stress positions'.

Over the next year, these coercive interrogation methods began to be used more widely. In August 2003,

Guantánamo's commander Major General Geoffrey Miller was dispatched to Iraq with a mandate to 'Gitmo-ize' ('Guantánamo-ise') the interrogation of suspected insurgents.[4] Miller recommended that prison guards be used to soften up detainees prior to interrogation,[5] and sent teams from Guantánamo to teach the 'enhanced' techniques.[6] But the rules determining which methods could be used, and who could authorise them, were rewritten several times during the following months.[7] This caused confusion among US troops about what their responsibilities were, and how far they could go in attempting to extract information.

Concerns about torture by US soldiers in Iraq came to a head in April 2004, with the publication of photographs depicting sadistic abuse at the Abu Ghraib detention centre. Guards were depicted forcing nude prisoners to pile on top of each other in 'human pyramids', dragging a naked inmate around on a leash, forcing detainees to simulate sex with each other, and posing with the corpses of prisoners who appeared to have been severely beaten.[8] Further pictures, unpublished at the time, showed male inmates being made to engage in homosexual acts, female prisoners forced at gunpoint to reveal their breasts, detainees being threatened with dogs,[9] and bloodied corpses of prisoners with gunshot wounds.[10]

A preliminary army investigation found 'numerous incidents of sadistic, blatant, and wanton criminal abuses'. Alongside the ill treatment that had been photographed, prisoners had been punched, slapped, kicked, beaten, attacked by dogs, threatened with guns and sodomised. President Bush condemned what he called the 'disgraceful conduct by a few American troops who dishonored our country and disregarded our values'.[11] The secretary of defence, Donald Rumsfeld, insisted that the abuses were 'an exceptional, isolated' case.

From Stanford to Abu Ghraib

When the soldiers involved in Abu Ghraib were put on trial, one of the witnesses for the defence was the Stanford psychologist Philip Zimbardo. It was Zimbardo who, more than 30 years earlier, had conducted the infamous Stanford prison experiment, in which an ordinary group of college students had been transformed within days into sadistic and abusive prison guards.

Testifying in the trial of Sergeant Ivan Frederick, Zimbardo argued that there were strong 'situational' pressures at Abu Ghraib that had been incredibly difficult to resist. Frederick had been responsible for over 1,000 Iraqi prisoners, twelve US army guards and 60 Iraqi policemen, and had worked in continual fear of insurgent attacks and prison riots. Prison guards had been made to work twelve-hour night shifts, seven days a week, often going for weeks on end without a break. Junior guards at Abu Ghraib had been told to create 'favourable conditions' for interrogations – with vague and conflicting instructions about what this meant. When Frederick had complained about the conditions, his concerns were dismissed and he was threatened with disciplinary action.

Zimbardo believes that the Abu Ghraib guards were 'trapped in a state of deindividualization. They could act and feel, but could not think'. Without proper training and supervision, many normal people placed in the same situation would have behaved as Frederick did. But this was more than just a bad case of work-related stress. What was really at fault, Zimbardo argued, was the command structure that had made the prison abuses possible.[12]

An official investigation by the former defence secretary James Schlesinger concluded that:

> The potential for abusive treatment of detainees ... was entirely predictable based on a fundamental understanding of the principles of social psychology coupled with an awareness of numerous known environmental risk factors. Most leaders were unacquainted with these ... factors, and therefore failed to take steps to mitigate the likelihood that abuses ... would occur during detainee operations.[13]

Schlesinger detailed a number of concepts used by psychologists to explain 'why individuals and groups who usually act humanely can sometimes act otherwise'. These included:

Deindividuation: ... the anonymity, suggestibility, and contagion provided in a crowd allows individuals to participate in behaviour marked by the temporary suspension of customary rules and inhibitions. Individuals within a group may experience reduced self-awareness which can also result in disinhibited behaviour.

Groupthink: ... symptoms of groupthink include: (1) illusion of invulnerability – group members believe the group is special and morally superior; therefore its decisions are sound; (2) illusion of unanimity in which members assume all are in concurrence, and (3) pressure is brought to bear on those who might dissent.

Dehumanization: ... individuals or groups are viewed as somehow less than fully human ...

Enemy image: ... both sides participating in a conflict tend to view themselves as good and peace-loving peoples, where the enemy is seen as evil and aggressive.

Moral exclusion: ... one group views another as fundamentally different, and therefore prevailing moral rules and practices apply to one group but not the other.[14]

Schlesinger noted that by their very nature, detention and interrogation involved one group wielding significant power over another. Such a relationship carried a 'higher risk of moral disengagement on the part of those in power', which without 'proper oversight and monitoring' was likely to lead to abuse.

Echoing Zimbardo, Schlesinger highlighted the pressures on the Abu Ghraib guards resulting from 'poor training … insufficient staffing, inadequate oversight, confused lines of authority ... internal threats from volatile and potentially dangerous prisoners and external threats from frequent mortar attacks'. He also concluded that the 'widespread practice of stripping detainees' may also have played a role:

> While the removal of clothing may have been intended to make detainees feel more vulnerable and therefore more compliant with interrogators, this practice is likely to have had a psychological impact on guards and interrogators as well. The wearing of clothes is an inherently social practice, and therefore the stripping away of clothing may have had the unintended consequence of dehumanising detainees in the eyes of those who interacted with them.

While in Zimbardo's experiment prisoners had been forced to cover their hair in order to accentuate the difference between them and their guards, in Abu Ghraib the prisoners were often hooded completely, reducing them almost literally to the status of a 'faceless' enemy. When our face is obscured, so too are our emotions – along with our most distinguishing physical features – and it becomes easier for others to see us as an anonymous member of a hated group.

The word 'compassion' has its roots in the Latin *com* (with) and *pati* (to suffer) – 'suffering with' another human being. It is far harder for others to 'suffer with' us – and far easier for them to inflict suffering on us – when the evidence of that suffering is hidden away behind a hood. Conversely, as the psychologist Stanley Milgram found with his electro-shock experiments in the 1960s, it's much harder to persuade someone to abuse another human being when they can see the victim's face.

It's difficult, too, to think of a more literal expression of moral exclusion – where we deem that 'prevailing moral rules and practices apply to one group but not the other' – than the concept of an 'unlawful combatant'. Those who fall under this label are defined as a wholly new kind of enemy to which 'new rules' apply, and who can be denied even the most basic of protections – the right to be free from torture – if 'military necessity' seems to justify it.

'The feeling among US soldiers I've spoken to in the last week is also that "the gloves are off"', one UK intelligence official reportedly told the *Guardian* in May 2004, shortly after the Abu Ghraib scandal broke. 'Many of them still think they are dealing with people responsible for 9/11.'[15]

'Bad apples'

The evidence that emerged after Abu Ghraib cast doubt on official assurances that the scandal was an isolated case. An internal investigation at the US army base in Mosul, the details of which were revealed in 2005, found that detainees were being 'systematically and intentionally mistreated'.[16] Inmates had been hit with water bottles, forced to exercise until they collapsed, subjected to deafening noise and deprived of sleep. Prisoners were not only hooded, but hooded 'with sandbags ... that were marked with different crimes, leading the guards to believe that the particular detainee committed that particular crime'.

The investigation had been triggered after one of the detainees, twenty-year-old Salah Salih Jassim, was hospitalised with a broken jaw. Jassim was not himself a suspect but had been arrested with his father, a former officer in the armed forces of the deposed Iraqi regime. He and several others were hooded with sandbags marked 'IED' – the standard acronym for 'Improvised Explosive Device', the roadside bombs that had claimed hundreds of American lives. 'They were setting it up to make the infantry guys angry', one witness told investigators; 'the guards were all over him, screaming at him things like "you like to use IEDs motherfucker", and smoking him extra'. Jassim had not only been dehumanised, he had literally been given a 'label' which identified him with one of the most despised weapons of the Iraqi insurgency.

At Forward Operating Base Tiger, near Al Qaim, newly arrived prisoners would be forced into a metal shipping container and deprived of sleep for 24 hours before being taken away for interrogation. In an interview with international campaign group Human Rights Watch, a US army interrogator, speaking under the pseudonym 'Nick Forrester', described the interrogation process:

> They'd sit you down on a chair. They start off with some softball questions, getting your name, getting warmed up, like that. And then, at the first 'no', at the first 'I don't know', at the first 'I don't have any information', the first wrong answer – that's when the lights went off … If [the detainee] was a particular target of interest that they thought knew something … they'd grab him, punch him – stomach, neck, arms – you know, right in here [indicating the back of the arm, above the elbow], you'd punch them in the back of the elbows – hold your arms up – you'd punch them in the back of the elbow, I guess, so not to leave a mark.

According to Forrester, every prisoner was subjected to some level of abuse, even when they were being wholly compliant – while those deemed uncooperative would be severely beaten. One of the worst cases involved a prisoner believed to have information about the Iraqi insurgency:

> He wouldn't say anything, and they kept screaming at him and screaming at him … They threw him up against the wall, they punched him in the neck, punched him in the stomach – you know, gut shot

191

... They hold [sic] his arms like this [out behind
his back] and then beat him down – enough so they
could break it ... Same with the kneecaps: kicked
him in the kneecaps, you know, really hard, with
those boots – combat boots.

It eventually became clear that the reason the detainee
wasn't answering was that he was Iranian, and spoke no
Arabic: 'He just kept getting the crap beat out of him
because they thought that he was being silent when he
only spoke Farsi ... they really thought this guy had a
bunch of information, and he never opened his mouth
except to scream incoherently, when he was getting hit.'

In 2004, 'Jeff Parry' (not his real name) worked as a
military interrogator at the secretive Camp Nama detention facility in Baghdad. In interviews with Human Rights
Watch, Parry later revealed how suspected insurgents had
routinely been deprived of sleep, bombarded with loud
music, stripped naked, doused with freezing water and
exposed to the elements in order to induce hypothermia.
'There was an authorization template on a computer,' Parry
told investigators, 'and it was a checklist ... it was all already
typed out for you, environmental controls, hot and cold,
you know, strobe lights, music, so forth. Working dogs,
which, when I was there, wasn't [sic] being used. But you
would just check what you want to use off, and if you
planned on using a harsh interrogation you'd just get it
signed off.'[17]

When Parry and a group of colleagues raised concerns about these methods with their commanding officer, they were called to a meeting at which military lawyers gave a two-hour PowerPoint presentation, explaining 'why this is necessary, why this is legal, they're enemy combatants, they're not POWs, and so we can do all this stuff to them and so forth'. The lawyers spelled out explicitly that the Geneva Conventions did not apply to the Camp Nama detainees, and that 'basically, we can do inhumane and degrading treatment'. Nonetheless, they insisted that the techniques were not actually inhumane, because 'they claim no lasting mental effects or physical marks or anything, or permanent damage of any kind'. When some soldiers voiced concerns that another legal authority might take a different view, leaving them open to prosecution, the lawyers insisted that they could not be held responsible – any punishment would come from the top down, and never reach them. When some raised worries about innocent Iraqis being caught up in the system with the 'unlawful combatants', they were told that 'we're in a new era ... we're in a war on terror, and these are things we have to do'.[18]

'Military necessity'

There's an argument for torture that goes something like this: what if a group of terrorists was plotting a series of devastating attacks against our major cities, aiming to kill thousands of civilians in pursuit of some deranged ideology? And what if we captured one of the top ring-leaders – and what if he was refusing to talk, despite our best efforts to get him to tell us what he knew? And what if, by using 'all means at our disposal', we could force him to reveal information that allowed us to prevent at least some of the attacks, thereby saving thousands of lives? Shouldn't torture be legal under those circumstances?

In the aftermath of the September 11th attacks, the 'ticking bomb' argument was one that many found seduc-tive. John Yoo, one of the White House legal advisers who had argued against upholding the Geneva Conventions in Afghanistan, later spelled out that 'this "military neces-sity" language has to do with the possibility that you have in your hands a terrorist leader who knows about attacks on the United States ... and you need to find that infor-mation to stop something you're afraid is going to happen in pretty short order'.[19]

It was Yoo who helped formulate the legal argument that US laws against torture only prohibit doing things that cause pain 'equivalent in intensity to the pain accom-panying serious physical injury, such as organ failure, impairment of bodily function, or even death'. Yoo has also maintained that, in extreme circumstances, the pres-ident would be permitted, under the US constitution, to disregard any law that Congress has ever passed, and autho-rise the severest of tortures in order to extract information.

The 'ticking bomb' argument falls within a school of

thought sometimes called consequentialism. Broadly speaking, anyone who believes that 'the end justifies the means' – that the right course of action is always the one that will produce the best (or least bad) outcome overall – is a consequentialist. Hard-line consequentialists argue that, in principle, any action, however brutal or cruel, can be justified if it is likely to bring about the 'greater good'.

The flip side of the 'ticking bomb' argument for torture is what we might call the 'ticking tyranny' argument for terrorism: what if a brutal regime were in power in your country, murdering thousands of innocent people each year, while thousands more starved to death due to economic mismanagement and rampant corruption? And what if, by launching a series of devastating terror attacks against the civilian population, you could weaken that regime enough to overthrow it, so that a more moderate government could take over, ending the cycle of violence? If all other options had failed, wouldn't it be right, in those circumstances, to massacre a few hundred innocent people in order to save thousands?

One answer to both of these arguments is to insist that human life has an absolute value – that it can never be right to play off the rights of one group of people against those of another, even if a million human lives are at stake. But sceptics can also put forward a more practical objection. All forms of ends-and-means morality seem to rely on the assumption that it is possible to know, in advance, what the precise consequences of one's actions are going to be. We may well be able to craft ourselves an imaginary scenario in which massacring 500 innocent people would trigger the downfall of a brutal government, thereby saving thousands of lives in the long term. But that isn't much good if it's impossible to know, in any given situation, that launching a terror campaign to bring down *this particular* brutal government will prove to be a successful strategy in this particular case – rather than, for example, providing the pretext for an even more vicious crackdown in which even more innocent people get killed.

Likewise, while we might feel less sympathy for a terror suspect facing torture than for an innocent civilian being targeted in a terrorist attack, the 'ticking bomb' argument faces similar practical problems. We may be able to conceive of an imaginary situation where we know with absolute certainty that the man we have captured really is a terrorist, and really does have information that really will save lives if we torture it out of him. But this isn't much good if, in reality, it's impossible to know with any certainty who we've captured, and what he knows – or what the overall consequences of our decision to torture him will be.

Within a modern judicial system, it can sometimes take years to establish, beyond reasonable doubt, whether or not a suspect is guilty of a serious crime – and even then miscarriages of justice sometimes happen. Yet the 'ticking bomb' scenario is premised on our being able to make this determination in a matter of hours. If we give the government the right to inflict torture merely on the basis of *suspicion*, then it seems inevitable that, even with the best of intentions, innocent people will end up getting caught up in the machine.

A report issued by the International Committee of the Red Cross (ICRC) in early 2004 noted that US officials were admitting that 70–90 per cent of those in custody in Iraq had been arrested by mistake. One army witness later told an internal investigation that 'the majority of our detainees were detained as the result of being in the wrong place at the wrong time ... swept up by Coalition Forces as peripheral bystanders during raids'. The witness estimated that only one in ten detainees were of 'intelligence value', but that there was nonetheless 'an extreme reluctance to release these low value inmates because of the fear that one of them might return to attack Coalition Forces'.[20] Janis Karpinski, Abu Ghraib's former commander, claims to have been told in the summer of 2003 that she should not release any more detainees, even if it was clear that they were innocent. Karpinski says that the order came from a senior major general, who told her: 'I don't care if we're holding 15,000 innocent civilians ... We're winning the war.'[21]

Once we have accepted that 'military necessity' can justify torture, it can be hard to resist applying the same logic to infringements that seem less brutal, such as pre-emptively interning thousands of people on the off-chance that some of them might have been planning to attack us. And once we have thousands of people in custody, some of whom we suspect may know something about the enemy we are fighting, it can be difficult to resist applying the logic of military necessity again, and authorising 'enhanced interrogation' for all of our detainees on the off-chance that this may yield some useful information.

In practice, the logic of 'ends and means' tends to entail a moral double standard almost by definition. To live a normal human life is precisely to see ourselves and our families as 'ends' rather than 'means' – something more than a tiny cog in a big machine, people whose thoughts, feelings, hopes and fears count for something in their own right, and who cannot simply be blown up, tortured or imprisoned in pursuit of some grand moral purpose. Yet when we apply the logic of ends and means, this is exactly the basic standard that we deny to others.

But perhaps the most fundamental problem with ends-and-means morality is that it requires us to have knowledge verging on omniscience about the likely consequences of our actions, while simultaneously pushing us towards a highly distorted view of reality. In order to commit brutal acts with a clear conscience, most normal people will need to subject themselves to heavy doses of delusion.

The conviction that we are a brave group of misunderstood visionaries, willing to do whatever it takes to save freedom, can be dangerously alluring. So too the notion that we can destroy our evil enemy with *just one more* act of brutality. By suppressing any doubts about the rightness of our cause, or the effectiveness of the methods being used, we can allay some of our guilt about the suffering we are causing, and take heart from the belief that we are making 'tough choices' for the greater good of humanity.

By demonising our perceived enemies as wholly and irredeemably evil, we allow ourselves to believe that the person being tortured or killed is not a human being like ourselves, but a hate-filled monster, devoid of goodness, who deserves the vicious treatment being meted out to them. And with the use of vague euphemisms, we can further disguise the true horror of what we are doing – both from others and from our own guilty consciences.

Most of us feel uncomfortable with the mental image of a small child being blown to pieces, or a man being shackled to a table and forcibly choked with water. To make these things sound more acceptable, we need to invent phrases specific enough to communicate the intended meaning, but bland enough to stop any nasty thoughts from arising in the process. This phenomenon was famously explored by George Orwell, writing shortly after the Second World War in his essay 'Politics and the English language':

> Defenceless villages are bombarded from the air, the inhabitants driven out into the countryside, the cattle machine-gunned, the huts set on fire with incendiary bullets: this is called *pacification*.

> Millions of peasants are robbed of their farms and sent trudging along the roads with no more than they can carry: this is called *transfer of population* or *rectification of frontiers*. People are imprisoned for years without trial, or shot in the back of the neck or sent to die of scurvy in Arctic lumber camps: this is called *elimination of unreliable elements*.[22]

Much of political language, Orwell argued back in 1946, was designed to 'make lies sound truthful and murder respectable, and to give an appearance of solidity to pure wind'. Subsequent decades have brought us the Vietnam war, and 'collateral damage' as a euphemism for civilian deaths; the war in Bosnia, with 'ethnic cleansing' in place of 'genocide'; and most recently of all the global 'war on terror', with its 'enhanced interrogation' in lieu of 'torture'.

But the more we distort our view of reality in order to allay guilt over our brutal actions, the more we undermine our ability to judge whether those actions really are bringing about the greater good. The need to believe that our violent means are achieving the end to which we are devoted can have us doggedly insisting that our harsh actions are 'working', even in the face of overwhelming evidence to the contrary. By immersing ourselves in bland, sanitised euphemisms, we diminish our ability to think things through for ourselves, and to confront the full reality of what we are doing. And by demonising the perceived threat, we inevitably exaggerate and oversimplify it, misrepresenting motives and limiting the chances of a non-violent resolution. The more we convince ourselves that our enemy is utterly unlike us, and utterly evil, the harder it is to find common ground on which to negotiate; it can begin to seem that we have no other option but to keep fighting until one side has exterminated the other. At the extreme, this can create a kind of 'feedback loop': in justifying our brutal actions, we create a more and more demonised view of our enemy while becoming increasingly paranoid and irrational as a result of that demonisation – which drives us in turn towards further brutality. In practice, playing profit and loss with innocent lives almost always leaves humanity in deficit.

The abuses committed within the 'war on terror' were limited, to some extent, by public pressure and by intervention from the US Senate and judiciary. Where such checks and balances are weak or non-existent – as in Cambodia under the Khmer Rouge regime during the 1970s – the paranoia can quickly become all-consuming. At the Tuol Sleng prison in the Cambodian capital Phnom Penh, Kang Khek Ieu – alias 'Comrade Duch' – oversaw the 'enhanced interrogation' of more than 17,000 of his compatriots. His job was to ensure that every prisoner made a full confession for their supposed crimes against the revolution – and then paid with their life.

'We saw enemies, enemies, enemies everywhere,' Duch told an interviewer 28 years later. 'Pol Pot, the Number

One Brother, said you always had to be suspicious, to fear something. And thus the usual request came: interrogate them again, interrogate them better.'[23]

Trial and error

When, in February 2003, the Thai government declared a 'war on drugs', one of the many rules discarded as obsolete was the stale old tradition of putting people on trial before you execute them. Long lists of criminal suspects were drawn up, and each regional police chief was given a target for the number of people to be arrested or 'extinguished' in his area. Within three months, an estimated 2,275 people had been gunned down in their homes or on the streets, including disproportionate numbers from ethnic minorities and several children.[24] Many were found dead soon after being summoned to their local police station. The official line was that these deaths were the result of rival drug dealers murdering each other or, in a handful of cases, police action in 'self-defence'.

The media seemed largely to approve, with TV soap stars sagely commenting that the government should use every method at their disposal to fight this terrible scourge, including, where necessary, 'extra-judicial means'. Later that year, working as a volunteer in Bangkok, I got a call from a young widow whose husband had been murdered. He'd been put on the blacklist by a disgruntled former business associate, and had last been seen being bundled into a car by local police. His wife insisted that he'd never had anything to do with drugs. I had no real way of telling whether or not this was true – but then, of course, without a criminal trial, neither did the Thai authorities.

Calls for due process to be respected are easily dismissed as 'soft', or even reckless. The terrorists don't give their victims a fair trial, the logic sometimes goes, so why should they deserve one themselves? The answer is that without such a trial, we don't know whether the person we've arrested really is guilty of what we suspect.

The rules that determine what government officials can and can't do are required not only to prevent abuses of power, but also to ensure that decisions are made on the basis of accurate information. The requirement that criminal cases must be proved 'beyond reasonable doubt' rather than merely 'on the balance of probabilities' isn't just about protecting the innocent from wrongful conviction. It also helps maintain the integrity of the system, by requiring that the police are as meticulous as possible in gathering and presenting evidence.

Likewise, the prohibition of torture is not just about being humane. Torture-tainted intelligence is notoriously unreliable; after a certain point, most of us will tell our tormentor whatever they want to hear. Basing key decisions on intelligence gained through torture can lead to catastrophic mistakes.

In a high-profile speech to the United Nations in

February 2003, US secretary of state Colin Powell announced disturbing evidence of links between Al Qaeda and the Iraqi government. An unnamed 'senior terrorist operative' had revealed that Iraq offered chemical and biological weapons training to Al Qaeda members over a number of years. One high-ranking militant had supposedly visited Iraq several times, 'for help in acquiring poisons and gases'.[25]

These same allegations were made repeatedly in the run-up to the March 2003 invasion – and contributed to an atmosphere in which the torture of Iraqis came to be seen as acceptable. It was only revealed much later that the 'terrorist operative' in question, Ibn al Shaykh al Libi, had made his WMD claims after being subjected to freezing temperatures and controlled drowning. In November 2005, CIA sources told ABC News that they had concluded that Libi 'had no knowledge of such training or weapons and fabricated the statements because he was terrified of further harsh treatment'.[26]

Caveat elector

It takes a certain kind of egoism to want to be a politician. The louder they claim it is because they 'want to make a difference', the tighter you should grip your wallet.

Paul Staines, www.order-order.com[27]

Given the disasters, human and financial, that can happen when governments lose their grip on reality, scepticism is arguably more important in politics than in any other area of life. Even when politicians aren't killing or torturing thousands of people, a lack of checks and balances can create plenty of opportunities for corruption. Expense accounts are fiddled, political decisions mysteriously reversed after generous donations from shady businessmen, and evidence of ministerial malfeasance withheld for 'security reasons'.

When a government brings in a law that gives more power to the general public – such as a new employment right or social benefit – legislators will generally look closely at how this right could be abused, in the worst case scenario, and ensure that measures are in place to stop such abuses happening. Anyone who tried to insist that such a safeguard was unnecessary, because the public could be trusted to behave honourably at all times, would likely be seen, at best, as something of an idealist.

Yet when politicians propose to give *themselves* more rights – be it the power to detain terror suspects without charge, ban demonstrations or use 'enhanced interrogation techniques' – the discussion often seems to unfold very differently. Concerns about the weakening of safeguards are countered with promises that the 'sweeping new powers' will only be used when strictly necessary, and always in a proportionate and responsible way. Underlying the discussion seems to be the assumption that government officials are inherently trustworthy, and that good intentions alone can ensure that the 'sweeping new powers' will not be abused or have unintended consequences. Yet the lesson of the global 'war on terror' seems to be that good intentions just aren't enough. Given human nature, it seems inevitable that the more broad powers we give to our public officials, the more mistakes and abuses will creep in.

In December 2005, a committed pacifist named Maya Evans was imprisoned for standing near the Cenotaph memorial and reading aloud the names of British soldiers who'd been killed in Iraq. In defending the new law, which banned demonstrations within one kilometre of Parliament without explicit police permission, Evans' MP Michael Foster argued that 'with the current terrorist threat it would be easy to mask a terrorist atrocity under the guise of a legitimate demonstration'.[28] Foster nonetheless expressed surprise that the new powers had been applied in such a heavy-handed way.

In the same month, the UK Foreign Office acted to block the publication of a series of memos written by Craig Murray during his time as Britain's ambassador to Uzbekistan. The documents clearly showed that the UK government was aware that intelligence received from the Uzbek police had been extracted through torture, undermining public assurances made by the then foreign secretary, Jack Straw.[29]

'Tortured dupes are forced to sign up to confessions showing what the Uzbek government wants the US and UK to believe', Murray had written to his bosses in July 2004.

'This material is useless ... It exaggerates the role, size, organisation and activity of the IMU [an Uzbek terror group]
and its links with Al Qaida. The aim is to convince the West
that the Uzbeks are a vital cog against a common foe, that
they should keep the assistance, especially military assistance,
coming, and that they should mute the international criticism on human rights ...'[30] The same memo recalled a March
2003 Foreign Office meeting at which the same issue had
been discussed. Murray had been told that his 'qualms of
conscience were 'respected and understood', but that the
torture-tainted material was 'very useful indeed'.

When Craig Murray sought to include the memo in
the book about his time as ambassador, *Murder in
Samarkand*, the Foreign Office threatened legal action,
claiming that his quoting of his own words would
constitute a breach of 'Crown copyright' and demanding
that he return all copies in his possession. But on this
occasion the unintended consequences of government
heavy-handedness were fairly benign: the policy wonks of
Admiralty Arch hadn't banked on the power of the internet.
Murray cried foul and posted the damning memo, along
with several others, to his website www.craigmurray.org.uk,
urging like-minded bloggers to copy it to their own pages.
Hundreds did, and the documents were soon widely
disseminated and discussed across the internet. At the time
of writing, two years later, Murray's site is still the first
that appears when you type the phrase 'damning documentary evidence' into Google.

Even a dry-sounding move to undermine an external check in the name of 'cutting red tape' can sometimes have serious consequences. Earlier in this book we saw how the emasculation of the independent Medicines Control Council in South Africa has seen a profusion of unproven drugs being marketed as treatments for Aids – some by companies with links to ruling-party officials. In 2006, the UK government pushed through the 'Legislative and Regulatory Reform Act',[31] which would have overturned centuries of tradition by granting cabinet ministers sweeping powers to rewrite laws without the approval of Parliament. The Act was passed by the House of Commons with only minor amendments; it was only when it reached the House of Lords that the most wide-ranging provisions were removed.[32]

Faced with a tide of sleaze and power-mongering, it can be tempting to retreat into cynicism, and conclude that politicians are a uniquely evil breed – liars and schemers all, bent on self-enrichment and self-advancement 'by any means necessary'. Yet this, too, is something of a caricature. While it seems likely, given the benefits on offer, that politics attracts more than its fair share of egoists and megalomaniacs, it is probably also true that most cases of corruption, abuse and self-delusion stem from human failings that we all share. It's just that dentists, traffic wardens, bus drivers and beauticians don't generally have the chance to do so much damage.

CONCLUSION

DON'T GET FOOLED AGAIN

Three days a week I take the train into the centre of London. A few minutes short of London Bridge, just after the Millwall stadium, I sometimes look over at the station on the parallel line. From here, South Bermondsey seems like little more than a thin platform, stilted precariously on a narrow embankment. In the mornings, a handful of commuters wait there like agitated birds on a telephone wire, and it's easy to imagine them being swept away by a gust of wind, or scattering in chaos as the line snaps beneath them.

I've passed that station many times since I began researching this book, and it's an image that has stayed with me as I've waded through the conspiracy theories, half-truths and finely-crafted rhetoric. From a certain angle, much of what passes for human knowledge can seem like educated guesswork at best – a flimsy platform perched on a windy embankment, carefully constructed but painfully fragile. When you're standing on that platform, it's impossible to see how thin it is, or how narrow the supports upon which it rests. And yet, once you've looked at things from afar, it can be hard to escape the feeling that the next gust might take the ground from underneath your feet. One logical flaw overlooked, one 'solid' piece of evidence that turns out to be hollow, and the whole structure could come crashing down.

But while some areas of human knowledge have been demolished and rebuilt countless times, others have been remarkably resilient, stubbornly holding out against the seismic shakes of history. Despite every attack on the foundations of rationality, the most basic principles of logic and evidence seem as sound today as when they were first committed to scrolls and tablets thousands of years ago.

In this book I've looked at a wide range of ideological delusions, from the seemingly benign to the manifestly crazed and reckless. Some have been built on decidedly shaky premises, while a few seem to hover miraculously in thin air. But in a sense they have all been variations on the same simple pattern. From the state-sponsored pseudo-science of Trofim Lysenko to the conspiracy theories of the '9/11 Truth Movement' and the depraved cultural relativism of Aids denial, all serve in some way to immunise the believer from against logic, or evidence, or both.

Fundamentalism asserts the absolute, literal truth of a particular set of beliefs. Whether contained in the written teachings of a religious text or the 'infallible' proclamations of a messianic cult leader, adherents deem these doctrines to be the highest form of truth available. Any evidence that conflicts with them must therefore be false by definition – and in some cases even the laws of logic are taken to be subordinate to the truths of the creed. However cruel or bizarre their beliefs, the religious zealot can always fall back on the defence that 'this is my faith'.

Relativism, in its most extreme form, is actually quite similar to fundamentalism: if doubt is the gap between belief and reality, then in asserting that belief *is* reality, we eliminate any room for doubt. Extreme relativism effectively abolishes logic by allowing both 'my truth' and 'your truth' to be true simultaneously, even when they contradict each other. Relativists are free to believe that Aids is a made-up disease, that the Holocaust didn't happen, or that their child has magical powers to see into the future, trumping any objection with the defence that 'this is what's true for me'. Milder forms of relativism leave logic in place, but allow the believer to dismiss any evidence he or she dislikes on the basis that it is 'socially constructed' or tainted by 'Western values'.

Conspiracy theories tend to accept logic, but reject conflicting evidence as automatically tainted by the conspirators and therefore false. Eyewitnesses are nothing more than paid stooges, documents all forgeries, and video evidence the product of CGI jiggery-pokery or a clever laser projection. The lack of concrete evidence in favour of the conspiracy claims, meanwhile, only goes to show the power and determination of the bad guys in covering up their evil deeds. But absence of evidence is not evidence of absence, the truth is out there, and those weapons of

211

mass destruction are still hidden away in the sand some-where; we just have to keep on digging.

Pseudo-scholarship gives the appearance of being based on logic and evidence, but relies instead on distortion, omission, fabrication, obfuscation, fallacy, emotive rhetoric and conspiracy theory. Quacks, cranks and fake historians seek to deceive by misrepresenting bad evidence as good, and using sham arguments to dismiss good evidence which conflicts with their own theories – often characterising themselves as 'sceptics' in the process. Some will have little or no academic training, relying instead on the classic con-man's tools of charm, charisma and the gift of the gab. Others may be genuine experts who have chosen to cash in on an established reputation in order to pursue some bogus agenda.

Pseudo-news may be the result of a simple fraud, as with the 1983 Hitler diaries forgery, and the 2006 hoax TV news report proclaiming the abolition of Belgium.[1] It may be that an individual journalist has been duped by a crank into thinking that they've unearthed a global 'conspiracy of silence' around a major political event, or a hitherto unpublicised scientific discovery. Or it may stem from a carefully orchestrated PR scam, like the manufactured 'controversy' over the link between smoking and cancer, or the 'honourable deception' over Iraqi WMDs in the run-up to the 2003 invasion.[2] But pseudo-news can often be the consequence when journalists repeat – without properly scrutinising the evidence – what they've been told by an off-the-record source, a PR agency, or a self-proclaimed 'expert'.

'I want to believe'

Most normal human beings, most of the time, can spot a delusional ideology when they see one. Yet time and again, intelligent and informed people are blinded to their better judgement. In order to protect ourselves from delusion, it's therefore also vital to be aware of the psychological 'blind spots' that can leave us vulnerable.

Wishful thinking is one of the defining features of human nature. We love to be told that we are 'special', that we have great prospects ahead of us, and that we are not to blame for our failings in life. At the same time, we often overestimate both our own power to control what goes on in the world, and that of our perceived enemies.

Over-idealisation stems from an exaggerated belief in our own specialness, and that of our social, cultural or ethnic group. A naive faith in the wisdom and goodness of our own people can blind us to the dangers of abuse, corruption and hubris. It can also leave us vulnerable to pseudo-theories that flatter our sense of racial or cultural superiority, or whitewash history in favour of our own side. At the extreme, an unquestioning attitude to our 'national myth', religion or political ideology can descend into a dangerous fundamentalism.

Demonising perceived enemies is the inverse of over-idealisation. If our own side is manifestly decent, wise and well-intentioned, then anyone who opposes us must surely be mad, bad or stupid. When we demonise an opponent, we blank out the good and imagine them to be wholly malevolent and inhumane. The belief in a dark and sinister enemy, bent on destroying or controlling us, can lead us to embrace conspiracy theories, together with the vain hope that by eliminating the bad guys we can remedy life's most fundamental ills.

Moral exclusion is often a by-product of demonisation. The idea that the enemy is fundamentally unlike us can encourage the belief that our moral standards do not apply to them. By seeing them as a faceless mass, rather than a collection of distinct individuals, it becomes easier to justify directing brutal acts against the group as a whole. At the extreme, moral exclusion can lead to indiscriminate violence, ranging from terrorism and torture to state-sanctioned genocide.

Groupthink results from a potent combination of psychological factors at work in close-knit social cliques. Through a strong sense of loyalty to our peers, deference to authority figures within the group, a demonised view of outsiders and a nagging fear of being excluded, we can start to develop a highly distorted view of reality. Any evidence that calls group assumptions into question is quickly rejected without proper evaluation. Bogus ideas that confirm group assumptions are accepted uncritically.

Doubters and dissenters are stereotyped as weak, disloyal or ill-intentioned.

Self-delusion begins at home

It's easy to demonise all those idiots who get bamboozled by the nonsense, and congratulate ourselves that we would never fall for anything so stupid. But if we do that, then we're much more likely to get fooled ourselves. The delusion that human nature operates differently for 'those idiots' than for us is perhaps the most dangerous one of all.

Myth and misconception are, to varying degrees, normal features of everyday human life. 'You can if you think you can' is a truly preposterous idea if treated as a statement of absolute, infallible, truth – but it can be a useful thing to think when you're struggling against some seemingly insurmountable psychological hurdle. We all need a bit of wishful thinking from time to time, to get ourselves to sleep at night or out of bed in the morning, or to psych ourselves up for some ghastly public speaking engagement. Perhaps the most important thing is to know which stones we are choosing to leave unturned, and know that this choice is benefiting us rather than leaving us open to exploitation.

Pigs, pokes and porkie-pies

The best way to cut through exploitative propaganda is to evaluate the evidence for yourself. When wide-eyed journalists are heralding a new scientific breakthrough based on 'the memory of water', or the government is warning of some devilish terror scheme to annihilate central London with nuclear-powered homing pigeons, we can usually learn a lot by getting on the internet and trying to track down the primary sources.

Is the evidence detailed and specific or vague and generalised? Does it come from multiple independent sources or just a handful? Is it internally coherent, or are there contradictions? Is it consistent with other well-supported facts? Are human sources named? If so, what are their credentials and what's their track record? Does the sum total of the available evidence support the conclusions that the government or the media is trying to draw? How difficult would it have been to fabricate this evidence?

This is no foolproof formula. It is possible to find plausible-sounding answers to all of these questions and still end up getting scammed. But by looking a bit more closely, we may at least cut down the risk and filter out some of the more egregious cases of bamboozlement. It is often surprising how easily a declaration that 'the evidence is overwhelming' or 'there is absolutely no doubt' can start to unravel when we do some simple fact checking.

Sometimes, however, we will go looking for the evidence and be told that, for some compelling reason, it cannot be revealed to us. This should set alarm bells ringing immediately. When politicians use terms like 'national security', 'commercial confidentiality', 'Crown copyright', 'the confidentiality of advice given by civil servants' and latterly 'MPs' privacy', this is sometimes nothing more than an eloquently worded gambit to evade public accountability.

Due to the very nature of official secrecy, it's difficult to put a percentage on exactly how often these trump-card excuses are being used to cover up abuse, dishonesty or incompetence. But from Tony Blair's 'pig in a poke' claim to have secret evidence proving that Iraq had weapons of mass destruction, to protestations from MPs that revealing how much public money they spend on expenses would violate their privacy,[3] it seems clear that we leave ourselves very vulnerable whenever we take such assurances at face value.

Experts, evidence, and evidence of expertise

Sometimes the evidence *will* be publicly available, and we won't be able to make head nor tail of it. This may be because it involves a lot of financial jargon, or because it's in Japanese, or because it's a microbiology paper about the characteristics of nucleoside reverse transcriptase inhibitors. In such cases, we can either try to become an expert in the subject ourselves, or we can look for an established authority who can decipher the evidence and explain it to us in layman's terms.

The obvious problem with option one is that even if we're willing to put in the work, we may just not be cut out for microbiology, advanced Japanese or a career in finance. Furthermore, no one can be a specialist in everything. All of us, at some point, will need to go with option two, and put our trust in an expert of one kind or another. Some classes of expert have a better track record than others, and the risks involved can vary greatly between professions. It seems doubtful, for example, that any major disasters have been caused in recent times by 'dodgy' Japanese translations, expert or otherwise. The record of the finance profession, on the other hand, is somewhat patchier. Many experts were comprehensively duped by the Enron scam in the late 1990s, and some members of the public lost out badly by following their advice.

Nucleoside reverse transcriptase inhibitors, meanwhile, may not sound like a whole bunch of fun, but as the leading group of anti-HIV drugs they are a matter of life or death to millions. And as so many Aids denialists have found in recent years, taking advice about them from the wrong sort of microbiologist can prove to be a deadly mistake.

There is, again, no failsafe formula to save us from the tomfoolery of pseudoscience. But there are some simple checks that can help: does this 'expert' have any genuine qualifications? Are they accredited by a recognised academic institution, or are they linked to a phoney institute with a dubious reputation? Do they have any criminal convictions? Have they ever published research in a peer-reviewed scientific journal? What do their peers say about them? Has any of their research, peer-reviewed or otherwise, ever been shown to be fraudulent? Have they actually done peer-reviewed research on the topic on which they are now seeking to comment?

In this book we've looked at several varieties of bogus expertise, each at a different point on the spectrum. At one extreme are Olga and Zigi Visser, the wholly unqualified purveyors of the wholly ineffective Aids drug, Virodene. At the other we have the work of Peter Duesberg, a well-respected virologist gone awry, who banked his reputation on a quixotic denial of the evidence linking HIV and Aids.[4]

It was partly through Duesberg's efforts that Neville Hodgkinson of the *Sunday Times* became so enthralled by Aids denialism during the early 1990s. Hodgkinson's articles gave an eloquent gloss, over several years, to Duesberg's insistence that the link between HIV and Aids was 'unproven', and perpetuated the misleading claim that Aids drugs were 'toxic'. To Hodgkinson, the fact that peer-reviewed medical journals refused to publish Duesberg's work was evidence not that his arguments might be flawed, but rather that a 'conspiracy of silence' was being perpetrated.

This use of an unsubstantiated conspiracy theory – or relativist socio-babble – to explain away a failure at the peer review stage is itself a giveaway sign of pseudoscience. In reality, without specialist knowledge of our own, our only reliable guide to the validity of a scientist's work has to be the consensus view among his or her peers. And if those peers have weighed the research in the balance and found it wanting, then unless we want to become experts ourselves, trying to dispute that consensus will be as futile as arguing over the finer points of Japanese grammar with a roomful of linguists from Okinawa.

Fear and loathing

Even at the best of times, we humans have a tendency to over-idealise ourselves, view our opponents through a stereotypical prism, and seek simplistic solutions to our problems. But our tendency towards 'black and white' thinking – and blind obedience – is greatly exaggerated when we feel stressed, insecure or physically endangered. One way to protect our sanity is to foster a healthy scepticism towards media scare-mongering and the politics of fear.

Anxiety sells newspapers, and this fact has triggered the growth of an industry dedicated to publicising every conceivable risk to our health or security, however improbable. But this relentless over-hyping can itself pose a danger to our health, and undermine our ability to think rationally. Media scares often absurdly exaggerate the risk from rare-yet-dramatic threats, such as terrorism, while trivialising more common dangers. In 2005, the year of the worst peacetime terror atrocity in modern British history, 100 times more Britons committed suicide than died at the hands of Al Qaeda, while many thousands more were killed by smoking-related diseases.

Politicians, too, have a vested interest in hyping the terrorist threat – stress and anxiety can make us far more willing to give our leaders 'sweeping new powers' in the hope that this will make the frightening thing go away. But as we saw in the last chapter, given human nature, it's inevitable that these sweeping powers, if left unchecked, will lead to corruption and abuse. The biggest danger of all is that our fear of the terrorist bogeyman will blind us to the misdeeds of those claiming to offer 'security', and provide a phoney pretext for ill-conceived military adventures. To date, many more British and American citizens have lost their lives fighting in Iraq than in terror attacks on their home nations. Intelligence agencies on both sides of the Atlantic have suggested that the war has actually increased the terrorist threat, rather than reducing it.[5]

One of the best antidotes to fear is laughter – and our leaders and leader-writers have certainly offered us some absurdities in the last few years. By mocking our fear-mongering political class and their torture-tainted nightmare tales, we not only bring some small measure of accountability to the political process – we can also help to counteract the anxiety culture that threatens both our health and our freedom.

Don't mourn, mobilise!

When we look at the checks and balances that help to

deter tomfoolery we tend to think in terms of formal institutions – the courts who prosecute corporate fraudsters, the lawmakers who scrutinise government policy, the peer-review panels who appraise scientific research, and the medical regulators who keep quack cures off the market. But in every society there is another, very different kind of 'balance' that is often ignored, sometimes bamboozled, frequently taken for granted, yet ever present nonetheless – the weight of public opinion.

Public opinion may be sidelined and circumvented, but this is one institution that can never be abolished – and you can't fool all of us all of the time. Furthermore, it has never been easier for private citizens to expose public deception, make their concerns heard, and join forces with others who feel the same way. And if we insist, loud enough and long enough, that we don't take kindly to being fooled – that our media and politicians need to start living by the same rules as the rest of us – it seems possible that the message will eventually be driven home.

Several years on from the 'dodgy dossier', governments continue to use spin, distortion and manipulation, and on occasions dispense with the truth entirely. It's hard to say whether our public officials tell *more* lies nowadays, or whether we've just got better at catching them. But until the costs of deception begin to outweigh the benefits, it seems inevitable that the lies will keep on coming.

While a police officer who fabricates evidence can be jailed for perjury, and a businesswoman who makes false claims about her products risks prosecution for fraud, there is no legal sanction against government ministers who tell porkie-pies in Parliament. And whereas I could sue my dentist for malpractice if he 'misread' my X-rays and gave me expensive root canal surgery without good cause, there is currently no mechanism for pursuing politicians who make disastrous military decisions on the basis of 'dodgy' intelligence.

In 2007, TV documentary-maker Richard Symons set about trying to tip the balance in favour of truth. Symons canvassed several prominent MPs to see if they would support a new law, the 'Misrepresentation of the People Act'. This would make it an offence for an elected politician to 'make or publish a statement which he knows to be misleading, false or deceptive in a material particular'.[6] The reaction was largely negative, with one member brusquely dismissing the very idea as 'naive'.[7] At the time of writing, just 37 MPs out of 646 had agreed to back it.

The standard objection was that a politician should be held to account through the ballot box: if we think they are fooling us, we can simply withhold our vote. But this seems equivalent to the only three shopkeepers in town insisting that our sole redress for the sale of duff goods should be a consumer boycott. In the face of all evidence to the contrary, our politicians continue to maintain that 'self-regulation' is enough to keep them honest. I, for one, am sceptical.

NOTES

CHAPTER ONE

1 'Blair's resignation speech in full', BBC News website, 10 May 2007, http://news.bbc.co.uk/1/hi/uk_politics/6642857.stm

2 'We're the best on earth, says upbeat PM', *The Age* online, 27 January 2007, http://www.theage.com.au/news/national/were-the-best-says-pm/2007/01/26/1169788693804.html

3 'The Language Police: Gettin' Jiggy with Frank Luntz', *Common Dreams*, 26 February 2005, http://www.commondreams.org/views05/0226-27.htm

4 P. Van Lange and C. Sedikides, 'Being more honest but not necessarily more intelligent than others: generality and explanations for the Muhammad Ali effect', *European Journal of Social Psychology*, 1998.

5 S.E. Taylor and J.D. Brown, 'Illusion and Well-Being: A Social Psychological Perspective on Mental Health', *Psychological Bulletin*, 1988. See also 'Optimists live longer', BBC News website, 8 February 2000 at http://news.bbc.co.uk/1/hi/health/635292.stm

6 C. Fine, *A Mind Of Its Own – How your brain distorts and deceives* (Icon, 2005), chapter 1, p. 24.

7 'Optimism Associated With Lowered Risk Of Dying From Heart Disease', ScienceDaily website, 4 November 2004, http://www.sciencedaily.com/releases/2004/11/041104011325.htm

8 'Is optimism the key to good health?', BBC News website, 2 January 2005, http://news.bbc.co.uk/1/hi/health/3481605.stm – see also 'Optimistic Attitudes Protect Against Progression of Carotid Atherosclerosis in Healthy Middle-Aged Women', http://www.psychosomaticmedicine.org/cgi/content/full/66/5/640#R15-1103

9   A. Jansen, T. Smeets, C. Martijn and C. Nederkoorn (Department
    of Experimental Psychology, University of Maastricht, The
    Netherlands), 'I see what you see: the lack of a self-serving body-
    image bias in eating disorders', *British Journal of Clinical
    Psychology*, March 2006, at
    http://www.ncbi.nlm.nih.gov/sites/entrez?cmd=Retrieve&db=pub
    med&dopt=AbstractPlus&list_uids=16480571&query_hl=3&itool
    =pubmed_docsum. The study concluded: 'Interestingly, the
    normal controls were the ones that showed a biased body image;
    they rated themselves far more attractive than other people rated
    them. These data suggest that the real problem in eating disor-
    ders is not a distorted body image but a lack of a distorted body
    image, that is, the lack of a self-serving body-image bias.'

10 C. Fine, op. cit., chapter 1, p. 24 – see also O. Burkeman,
    'Depressive realism', *Guardian*, 25 November 2006, http://lifeand-
    health.guardian.co.uk/wellbeing/story/0,,1954393,00.html

11 J.D. Taylor and S.E. Brown, 'Illusion and Well-Being: A Social
    Psychological Perspective on Mental Health', *Psychological Bulletin*
    (American Psychological Association, 1988), vol. 103, no. 2,
    http://imagesrvr.epnet.com/embimages/pdh2/bul/bul1032193.pdf

12 C. Fine, op. cit., chapter 1, p. 6.

13 D. Fronkin, 'Best escape: the end was near', *New York Times*, 18
    April 1999,
    http://query.nytimes.com/gst/fullpage.html?res=9B03EED91E39F9
    3BA25757C0A96F958260

14 R. McNamara, *In Retrospect: The Tragedy and Lessons of Vietnam*
    (Vintage, 1996).

15 Extract from R. McNamara, op. cit., p. 527, in *The American
    Journal of International Law*, vol. 90, no. 3 (July 1996), at
    http://links.jstor.org/sici?sici=0002-
    9300(199607)90%3A3%3C527%3AIRTTAL%3E2.0.CO%3B2-P

16 'The Mayor's Response to the London Assembly', website of the
    Mayor of London, 22 February 2005, at
    http://www.london.gov.uk/mayor/mayor_letter_220205.jsp – see
    also Lord Rothermere, *Daily Mail*, 10 July 1933: 'There has been
    a sudden expansion of their national spirit like that which took

place in England under Queen Elizabeth. Youth has taken command ... It would be both futile and unfair to resent this revival of German spirit. Each nation has the right to make the most of its own resources. It is Germany's good fortune to have found a leader who can combine for the public good all the most vigorous elements in the country.' Quoted in F. Kempe, *Father/Land – A Personal Search for the New Germany*, extract published in *New York Times*, 11 July 1999, http://www.nytimes.com/books/first/k/kempe-land.html

17 J. Carey, *The Times*, 6 March 2005, review of M. Pugh, *Hurrah for the Blackshirts* (Cape, 2005), http://entertainment.timesonline.co.uk/tol/arts_and_entertainment/books/article416895.ece

18 L. Sheeter, 'Ukraine remembers famine horror', BBC News website, 24 November 2007, http://news.bbc.co.uk/1/hi/world/europe/7111296.stm

19 Letter from G.B. Shaw, 'Social Conditions in Russia – Recent Visitor's Tribute', *Manchester Guardian*, 2 March 1933, see http://www.garethjones.org/soviet_articles/bernard_shaw.htm – see also W. Bennett, 'How Shaw defended Stalin's mass killings', *Daily Telegraph*, 18 June 2003, http://www.telegraph.co.uk/news/main.jhtml?xml=/news/2003/06/18/nshaw18.xml&sSheet=/news/2003/06/18/ixhome.html

20 C. Rawson, 'Playwright pleasant and unpleasant', *New York Times*, 20 October 1991, http://query.nytimes.com/gst/fullpage.html?res=9D0CE2D9123AF933A15753C1A967958260&sec=&spon=&pagewanted=all

21 http://www.nytimes.com/books/98/05/10/specials/mailer-abbot.html

22 'Norman Mailer' (obituary), *The Times*, 12 November 2007, http://www.timesonline.co.uk/tol/comment/obituaries/article2852134.ece

23 'In the mind, and the belly of the beast', *Independent*, 19 February 2002, http://findarticles.com/p/articles/mi_qn4158/is_20020219/ai_n12598976

24 'Norman Mailer' (obituary), *The Times*, 12 November 2007,
   http://www.timesonline.co.uk/tol/comment/obituaries/article2852
   134.ece

25 M. Gado, 'Jack Abbott – murderer made into literary celebrity:
   The Trial', *Crime Library*, undated, at
   http://www.crimelibrary.com/notorious_murders/celebrity/jack_a
   bbott/9.html

26 M. Gado, 'Jack Abbott – murderer made into literary celebrity:
   The Trial', *Crime Library*, undated, at
   http://www.crimelibrary.com/notorious_murders/celebrity/jack_a
   bbott/12.html

27 D. Robson, 'The gang's all here for last of Krays', *Daily Express*, 12
   October 2000,
   http://www.bernardomahoney.com/forthcb/krays/articles/tgah-
   flok.shtml

28 'You can't be a sweet cucumber in a vinegar barrel: A talk with
   Philip Zimbardo', *The Edge*, 19 January 2007,
   http://www.edge.org/3rd_culture/zimbardo05/zimbardo05_index.
   html

29 P. Zimbardo, Stanford prison experiment website,
   http://www.prisonexp.org/

30 'Strip-Search Case Victim Awarded $6.1 Million', ABC News
   website, 5 October 2006,
   http://abcnews.go.com/2020/story?id=3688563&page=1

31 'Milgram's Progress', *American Scientist*, July–August 2004,
   http://www.americanscientist.org/template/BookReviewTypeDetail
   /assetid/34009;jsessionid=aaa6R5S4PzyPgf

32 K. Millis, North Illinois University Psychology Department,
   'Stanley Milgram',
   http://www3.niu.edu/acad/psych/Millis/History/2003/
   stanley_milgram.htm#Biography

33 S. Milgram, 'The Perils of Obedience', *Harpers Magazine*, 1974,
   http://www.harpers.org/archive/1973/12/0021874 – also archived
   at http://www.paulgraham.com/perils.html

34 Ibid.

35 B. Weiner, *Judgements of Responsibility – A foundation for a theory*

of social conduct, (Guilford Press, 1995), p. 42,
http://books.google.co.uk/books?id=E_50yBklCI4C&pg=PA42&lpg=PA42&dq=%22i+only+said+i+was+the+greatest+not+the+smartest%22&source=web&ots=0H6S_C1Nln&sig=_UxewCva3UoEVxxptLxDX4c-HfM&hl=en

36 This investigation became the subject of my book *Titanic Express* (London: Continuum, 2006).

37 Plato (trans. R. Waterfield), *Gorgias* (Oxford: Oxford University Press, 1994), p. 24, http://books.google.co.uk/books?id=-aBLtSbDWTsC&pg=PA24&lpg=PA24&dq=%22rhetoric+is+the+only+area+of+expertise+you+need+to+learn+you+can+ignore+all+the+rest+and+still+get+the+better+of+the+professionals%22&source=web&ots=7MeN_TQFMc&sig=aTEbWMn3RPZggVzcHZ7-05S_LxA&hl=en

38 *Holy Bible*, King James Version, at http://bible.cc/john/20-29.htm

39 E. Magnuson, 'Hitler's forged diaries', *Time* magazine, 16 May 1983, http://www.time.com/time/magazine/article/0,9171,925946,00.html

40 'Hitler's Diaries: Real or Fake?', *Time* magazine, 9 May 1983, http://www.time.com/time/magazine/article/0,9171,923630-3,00.html

41 '1983: "Hitler diaries" published', BBC News website, 'On This Day' entry for 25 April 1983, http://news.bbc.co.uk/onthisday/hi/dates/stories/april/25/newsid_4464000/4464109.stm

42 'Faked books follow long tradition of literary swindles', *The Age* online, 7 March 2008, http://news.theage.com.au/faked-books-follow-long-tradition-of-literary-swindles/20080307-1xu2.html

43 D. Bilefsky, 'Outrage in Belgium after television broadcast hoax', *International Herald Tribune*, 14 December 2006, http://www.iht.com/articles/2006/12/14/news/belgium.php

44 'Viewers fooled by "Belgium split"', BBC News website, 14 December 2006, http://news.bbc.co.uk/1/hi/world/europe/6178671.stm

CHAPTER TWO

1 Urbina, 'This war brought to you by the Rendon Group', *Asia Times*, 13 November 2002,
   http://www.atimes.com/atimes/Middle_East/DK13Ak01.html

2 'Iraq Cited for Numerous Rights Violations in Kuwait', Amnesty International report, 20 December 1990, http://www.globalsecurity.org/wmd/library/news/iraq/1990/901220-166247.htm

3 P. Knightley, 'The disinformation campaign', *Guardian*, 4 October 2001, http://www.guardian.co.uk/Archive/Article/
   0,4273,4270014,00.html

4 Ibid. See also I. Urbina, 'This war brought to you by the Rendon Group', *Asia Times*, 13 November 2002,
   http://www.atimes.com/atimes/Middle_East/DK13Ak01.html

5 J. MacArthur, 'Remember Nayirah, Witness for Kuwait?', *New York Times*, 6 January 1992, http://www.hbo.com/films/livefrom-baghdad/related.shtml

6 L. Komisar, 'Truth in the Crossfire – "Live From Baghdad" Peddles Lie', *Pacific News Service*, 2 December 2002,
   http://news.pacificnews.org/news/view_article.html?article_id=223
   76a4a351c6dd2c433a8a527780ac7

7 'Deception on Capitol Hill', *New York Times*, 15 January 1992,
   http://query.nytimes.com/gst/fullpage.html?res=9E0CEEDD1338F
   936A25752C0A964958260

8 Ibid.

9 A.E. Rowse, 'How to build support for war', *Columbia Journalism Review*, September/October 1992,
   http://backissues.cjrarchives.org/year/92/5/war.asp

10 'Hill and Knowlton – a corporate profile', *Sourcewatch*, June 2002,
   http://www.corporatewatch.org.uk/?lid=380#humanrights

11 Ibid.

12 A.E. Rowse, 'How to build support for war', *Columbia Journalism Review*, September–October 1992,
   http://backissues.cjrarchives.org/year/92/5/war.asp

13 T. Regan, 'When contemplating war, beware of babies in incubators', *Christian Science Monitor*, 6 September 2002,

http://www.csmonitor.com/2002/0906/p25s02-cogn.html

14 Ibid.

15 'How PR sold the war in the Persian Gulf', PRwatch website (Center for Media and Democracy), undated, http://www.prwatch.org/books/tsigfy10.html

16 L. Marano, 'Propaganda: Remember the Kuwaiti babies?', *United Press International*, 26 February 2002, http://www.upi.com/NewsTrack/Quirks/2002/02/26/propaganda_r emember_the_kuwaiti_babies/6084/

17 'A Debate on One of the Most Frequently Cited Justifications for the 1991 Persian Gulf War: Did PR Firm Hill & Knowlton Invent the Story of Iraqi Soldiers Pulling Kuwaiti Babies From Incubators?', *Democracy Now*, 2 December 2003, http://www.democracynow.org/2003/12/2/a_debate_on_one_of_the

18 S. Peterson, 'In war, some facts less factual', *Christian Science Monitor*, 6 September 2002, http://www.csmonitor.com/2002/0906/p01s02-wosc.htm

19 N. Davies, 'Our media have become mass producers of distortion', *Guardian* Comment is Free website, 4 February 2008, http://www.guardian.co.uk/commentisfree/story/ 0,,2251982,00.html

20 http://www.cipr.co.uk/direct/careers.asp?v1=careers

21 http://www.prospects.ac.uk/cms/ShowPage/Home_page/ Explore_job_sectors/Advertising__marketing_and_PR/ overview/p!elpkXe

22 'CEBR – The Economic Significance of Public Relations', by the Centre for Economics and Business Research, Media Standards Trust website, November 2005, http://www.mediastandardstrust.org/resources/mediaresearch/rese archdetails.aspx?sid=1263

23 'PRchitecture', Gyroscope Consultancy website, undated, http://www.gyroscopeconsultancy.com/why.html

CHAPTER THREE

1 'What Hill and Knowlton can do', Letters, *New York Times*, 28 October 1990, http://query.nytimes.com/gst/ full-page.html?res=9C0CEEDF1230F93BA15753C1A966958260 – see also E. Press, 'The Suharto lobby', May 1997, http://www.etan.org/issues/older/suhlobby.htm

2 D. Turner, 'Hill & Knowlton revives by sprucing up its own image', *Los Angeles Business Journal*, 28 July 1997, http://findarticles.com/p/articles/mi_m5072/is_n30_v19/ai_19949797

3 J. Hood, 'PR role grows as Enron tries to rebuild', *PR Week*, 1 July 2002, http://www.prweekus.com/PR-role-grows-as-Enron-tries-to-rebuild/article/44636/

4 S.B. Trento, 'Lord of the lies; how Hill and Knowlton's Robert Gray pulls Washington's strings', *Washington Monthly*, September 1992, http://findarticles.com/p/articles/mi_m1316/is_n9_v24/ai_12529888/pg_7

5 F. Rich, 'State of the Enron', *New York Times*, 2 February 2002, http://query.nytimes.com/gst/fullpage.html?res=9507E5DD153DF931A35751C0A9649C8B63

6 P. Brogan, 'The Torturers' Lobby – How Human Rights Abusing Nations are Represented in Washington', Center for Public Integrity, Washington, 1992, http://www.publicintegrity.org/docs/torturers_lobby.pdf – page 7 of the report lists Kuwait, China, Turkey, Peru, Israel, Egypt, Republic of Angola and Indonesia as clients of Hill and Knowlton.

7 G. Monbiot, 'Who really belongs to another age – bushmen or the House of Lords?', *Guardian*, 21 March 2006, http://www.guardian.co.uk/commentisfree/2006/mar/21/comment.politics

8 'Western PR company to sell Uganda', BBC News website, 19 May 2005, http://news.bbc.co.uk/1/hi/world/africa/4563909.stm

9 P. Foster, 'Maldives dictator tries a touch of New Labour spin', *Daily Telegraph*, 17 June 2006, http://www.telegraph.co.uk/news/main.jhtml?xml=/news/2006/06/

17/wmaldives117.xml&sSheet=/news/2006/06/17/ixnews.html

10 G. Monbiot, op. cit.

11 A. Mundy, 'Is the Press any match for powerhouse P.R.?',
    Columbia Journalism Review, September/October 1992,
    http://backissues.cjrarchives.org/year/92/5/pr.asp

12 The story of the tobacco industry's efforts to conceal and distort
    the scientific consensus over smoking and cancer are laid out in
    magisterial detail by Harvard medical historian Allan M. Brandt,
    in his book *The Cigarette Century: The Rise, Fall, and Deadly
    Persistence of the Product that Defined America* (Basic Books,
    2007).

13 R.N. Proctor, 'Tobacco and Health – Expert Witness Report Filed
    on behalf of Plaintiffs in *The United States of America, Plaintiff, v.
    Philip Morris, Inc., et al., Defendants*, Civil Action No. 99-CV-
    02496 (GK) (Federal Case)', in *Journal of Philosophy, Science and
    Law*, vol. 4, March 2004,
    http://www6.miami.edu/ethics/jpsl/archives/papers/tobacco.html

14 Two landmark epidemiological studies were both published in
    1950: E. Graham and E. Wynder, 'Tobacco smoking as a possible
    etiologic factor in bronchiogenic carcinoma: a study of 684
    proven cases', *Journal of American Medicine*; and R. Doll and A.
    Bradford-Hill, 'Smoking and Carcinoma of the Lung: Preliminary
    Report', *British Medical Journal*, both of which are discussed in
    A.M. Brandt, op. cit., chapter 5, pp. 131–53.

15 A.M. Brandt, op. cit., chapter 5, pp. 153–57.

16 'Memorandum from T.V. Hartnett', 15 December 1953,
    http://legacy.library.ucsf.edu/tid/gvp34e00/ – discussed in A.M.
    Brandt, op. cit., chapter 6, p. 165.

17 B.C. Goss, 'Background material on the cigarette industry client',
    15 December 1953, http://legacy.library.ucsf.edu/tid/ufu91f00/,
    discussed in A.M. Brandt, op. cit., chapter 6, p. 166.

18 Letter from John Hill to Clarence Cook Little, 15 July 1954,
    http://tobaccodocuments.org/ness/3898.html – discussed in A.M.
    Brandt, op. cit., chapter 6, p. 191.

19 Tobacco Industry Research Committee, 'A Frank Statement To
    Cigarette Smokers', 4 January 1954,

http://www.tobacco.org/History/540104frank.html

20 D. Janson, 'End to suit denied in smoking death', *New York Times*, 22 April 1988, http://query.nytimes.com/gst/fullpage.html?res=940DEEDC153AF 931A15757C0A96E948260

21 'Confidential Report – Tobacco Industry Research Committee Meeting', 19 October 1954, http://tobaccodocuments.org/ctr/CTRMN007295-7297.html – discussed in A.M. Brandt, op. cit., chapter 6, p. 175.

22 A.M. Brandt, op. cit., chapter 6, p. 176 – see also 'Urges Sterilization of Mental Defectives; University of Michigan President Also Advocates Birth Control for Poor', *New York Times*, 19 November 1925, http://select.nytimes.com/gst/abstract.html?res=FB0F13F9385D1A 728DDDA00994D9415B858EF1D3&scp=26&sq=clarence+cook+li ttle&st=p

23 Tobacco Industry Research Committee, *Tobacco Industry Research Committee Press Conference* (condensed transcript), 15 June 1954, http://legacy.library.ucsf.edu/tid/ryd6aa00 – discussed in A.M. Brandt, op. cit., chapter 6, p. 175.

24 A.M. Brandt, op. cit., chapter 6, p. 181.

25 Ibid., p. 176.

26 Ibid., p. 181.

27 E.L. Wynder, 'An appraisal of the smoking–lung cancer issue', *New England Journal of Medicine*, 15 June 1961, http://tobac- codocuments.org/lor/00325507-5514.html – discussed in A.M. Brandt, op. cit., chapter 6, p. 205.

28 Clarence Cook Little, 'Some phases of the problem of smoking and lung cancer', *New England Journal of Medicine*, 15 June 1961, http://tobaccodocuments.org/lor/00325507-5514.html – discussed in A.M. Brandt, op. cit., chapter 6, p. 176.

29 A.M. Brandt, op. cit., chapter 6, p. 176.

30 Earl Newsom and Company, *Annual Reports of the Council for Tobacco Research*, 21 December 1972, http://legacy.library.ucsf.edu/tid/hah70a00/pdf – discussed in A.M. Brandt, chapter 6, p. 189.

31 'TIRC Funds For Smoking Research Now Over $2,000,000',
    Tobacco and Health (industry-funded publication), January–
    February 1958, http://legacy.library.ucsf.edu/tid/utg70a00/pdf

32 A.M. Brandt, op. cit., chapter 6, p. 182.

33 Ibid., pp. 186–7.

34 Ibid., p. 191.

35 Ibid., p. 194.

36 Clarence Cook Little, 'Statement requested from CCL by Doctor
    Rienhoff in phone conversation 11/4/54', 5 November 1954 –
    'Doctors Ochsner and Graham, who wrote the foreword to
    Doctor Ochsner's book, have long been regarded as the foremost
    and most vociferous medical, anti-tobacco propagandists.'
    http://tobaccodocuments.org/ness/3886.html – discussed in A.M.
    Brandt, op. cit., chapter 6, p. 191.

37 A.M. Brandt, op. cit., p. 195.

38 Ibid., chapter 6, p. 194.

39 Ibid., chapter 6, p. 185.

40 Ibid., chapter 6, p. 198.

41 Ibid., chapter 7, p. 227.

42 Ibid., chapter 6, p. 161.

43 Ibid., chapter 6, p. 184.

44 G. Ross, 'The Bookshelf talks with Allan M. Brandt', *American
    Scientist*, 7 June 2007,
    http://www.americanscientist.org/template/InterviewTypeDetail/as
    setid/55551

45 A. Mundy, 'Is the Press Any Match for Powerhouse PR?',
    Columbia Journalism Review, September–October 1992,
    http://backissues.cjrarchives.org/year/92/5/pr.asp

46 http://www.asbestos-institute.ca/

47 'Connecting the dots', *British Asbestos Newsletter*, issue 48,
    autumn 2002, http://www.lkaz.demon.co.uk/ban48.htm

48 S. Rampton and J. Stauber, 'Monsanto and Fox: Partners in
    Censorship', *PR Watch newsletter*, second quarter, 1998,
    http://www.prwatch.org/prwissues/1998Q2/foxbgh.html:
    'Is this an example of local TV's growing reluctance to air
    hard-hitting investigative news pieces?' asked Eric Deggans of the

St Petersburg Times before concluding that 'The truth, as always, lies somewhere in the middle.'

See also J. Davis, 'No one swallows this tax propaganda', *Independent*, 12 April 1997, http://findarticles.com/p/articles/mi_qn4158/is_19970412/ai_n14115135:

'Labour tells us that the typical family has paid more than £2,000 in extra taxes since 1992, while the Tories say that the average family is £1,100 a year better off than at the time of the last election ... The truth as always lies somewhere in the middle.'

And B. Johnson, 'Listening goes legit', *Guardian*, 10 November 2003, http://arts.guardian.co.uk/netmusic/story/0,,1081853,00.html:

'The truth, as always, is likely to be somewhere in the middle of these two contrary positions. One thing, though, is certain: file sharing is unlikely to disappear.'

CHAPTER FOUR

1 'DR Congo children "still armed"', BBC News website, 11 October 2006, http://news.bbc.co.uk/1/hi/world/africa/6039162.stm

2 'More children killed on UK roads', BBC News website, 28 June 2007, http://news.bbc.co.uk/1/hi/uk/6248552.stm

3 T. Kirby and A. Malone, 'Terror comes to London: More than 50 died in worst attack since Second World War', *Independent*, 8 July 2005, http://www.independent.co.uk/news/uk/crime/terror-comes-to-london-more-than-50-died-in-worst-attack-since-second-world-war-497929.html – see also 'In Depth – London attacks', BBC News website, undated, http://news.bbc.co.uk/1/hi/in_depth/uk/2005/london_explosions/default.stm

4 Mind, 'Suicide rates, risks and prevention strategies', accessed 6 March 2008, http://www.mind.org.uk/Information/Factsheets/Suicide/ – and

'International Suicide Prevention Awareness Week', website of the Scottish Government, 4 September 2006, http://www.scotland.gov.uk/News/Releases/2006/09/04165204. According to these sources, in 2005 there were 4,336 suicides in England and Wales, and 763 in Scotland, totalling 5,099.

5 'Tobacco', UK Department of Health website, accessed 8 March 2008, http://www.dh.gov.uk/en/Publichealth/Healthimprovement/Tobacco/index.htm – the Department of Health estimates that 106,000 people die from a smoking-related illness in the UK every year.

6 T. Varadarajan, 'Bad Company – Rupert Murdoch and his son genuflect before Chinese communists', *Wall Street Journal*, 26 March 2001, http://opinionjournal.com/columnists/tvaradarajan/?id=85000753 – see also M. Calderone, 'Top Murdoch Critic Flees *Journal*', *New York Observer*, 14 September 2007, http://www.observer.com/2007/top-murdoch-critic-flees-journal

7 'Patten sues over scrapped book deal', BBC News website, 27 February 1998, http://news.bbc.co.uk/1/hi/uk/60781.stm– see also 'Why Murdoch killed Patten book', *Telegraph*, 27 February 1998, http://www.telegraph.co.uk/htmlContent.jhtml?html=/archive/1998/02/27/npat27.html

8 'Media Backtalk', online discussion with Howard Kurtz, *Washington Post* website, 6 August 2007, http://www.washington-post.com/wp-dyn/content/discussion/2007/08/02/DI2007080201869.html

9 An annotated version of the programme transcript, together with the reporters' comments on the disputed edits, is available at this website: http://www.foxbghsuit.com/exhibit%20q.htm – J. Acre and S. Wilson, 'The Mystery In Your Milk – As Mandated by Fox 13 Management/Legal Counsel – Script 1, Version 28', *BGH Bulletin*, undated

10 This case is discussed in detail in chapter 7 of *The Silent Takeover* by Noreena Hertz (Arrow Books, 2002), and is also featured in the 2003 documentary *The Corporation*, by Mark Achbar, Jennifer Abbott and Joel Bakan –http://www.thecorporation.com,

reviewed at http://film.guardian.co.uk/News_Story/
Critic_Review/Observer_Film_of_the_week/0,,1339934,00.html –
P. French, 'In the companies of wolves', *Observer*, 31 October
2004. At the time of writing, the documentary could be viewed
in full at http://www.archive.org/details/thecorporationMP4, with
excerpts featuring Akre and Wilson available at
http://www.youtube.com/watch?v=9E-5KivgwO4

11 *'New World Communications v. Jane Akre* – Case No. 2D01-529',
District Court of Appeal of Florida, Opinion filed 14 February
2003,
http://www.2dca.org/opinion/February%2014,%202003/2D01-
529.pdf – see also K. Drum, 'We Report, You Decide …',
Washington Monthly website, 9 March 2003,
http://www2.washingtonmonthly.com/archives/individual/2003_0
3/000620.php

12 'Under the influence', *Editor's Notes*, American Society of
Business Publications, 9 October 2003,
http://www.folioshow.com/images/uploads/SpeakerPresentations/
EditorialSuttonNorth/M145EditorialEthics.pdf

13 J.I. Chainon, 'Newsroom priorities, Threat to Independence', The
Editors Weblog, The World Editors Forum, 27 March 2007,
http://www.editorsweblog.org/analysis/2007/03/4_newsroom_prio
rities_threats.php

14 S. Goldberg, 'Bush payola scandal deepens as third columnist
admits being paid', *Guardian*, 29 January 2005,
http://www.guardian.co.uk/media/2005/jan/29/pressandpub-
lishing.usnews

15 M. Woolf, 'Scruton sacked by second newspaper for tobacco
links', *Independent*, 5 February 2002,
http://findarticles.com/p/articles/mi_qn4158/is_20020205/ai_n125
97764

16 M. Woolf and D. Lister, 'Scruton likely to lose newspaper columnist job after exposure of financial link to tobacco firm',
Independent, 25 January 2002,
http://www.independent.co.uk/news/media/scruton-likely-to-lose-
newspaper-columnist-job-after-exposure-of-financial-link-to-

tobacco-firm-668171.html

17 R. Scruton, 'The Gothenburg street fighters were driven to violent protest', *Telegraph*, 19 June 2001, http://www.telegraph.co.uk/opinion/main.jhtml?xml=/opinion/20 01/06/19/do01.xml

18 R. Scruton, 'WHO abrogating responsibilities, exceeding authority', Institute of Economic Affairs website, May 2000, http://www.iea.org.uk/record.jsp?type=release&ID=3

19 T. Blacker, 'A minor sin in the media whorehouse', *Independent*, 29 January 2002, http://findarticles.com/p/articles/mi_qn4158/is_20020129/ai_n966 9841

20 http://www.mediastandardstrust.com/

21 http://www.fair.org

22 http://www.sourcewatch.org

23 http://www.publicintegrity.org/

24 http://www.rsf.org/

25 http://www.indexoncensorship.org/

26 http://www.pressgazette.co.uk/

CHAPTER FIVE

1 These include: C. Booker, 'Billions to be spent on nonexistent risk', *Sunday Telegraph*, 13 January 2002 – http://www.telegraph.co.uk/news/uknews/1381270/Christopher-Booker%27s-Notebook.html and C. Booker, '"Unnecessary" asbestos bill will top £8bn', *Telegraph*, 27 January 2002, http://www.telegraph.co.uk/news/1382802/Christopher-Booker%27s-Notebook.html

See also:

J. Monks, 'No evidence to say fibre is safe', Letters, *Daily Telegraph*, 3 February 2002, http://www.telegraph.co.uk/opinion/main.jhtml?xml=/opinion/20 02/02/03/dt0304.xml

'HSE confirms white asbestos remains a threat', Health and Safety Executive website, 5 February 2002, http://www.hse.gov.uk/press/2002/e02010.htm

C. Booker, 'The great asbestos cull begins', *Sunday Telegraph*, 10 February 2002, http://www.telegraph.co.uk/news/uknews/1384329/Christopher-Booker%27s-Notebook.html

Timothy Walker (Director General of the Health and Safety Executive), 'Booker's claims are irresponsible', *Telegraph*, 17 February 2002, http://www.telegraph.co.uk/opinion/main.jhtml?xml=/opinion/2002/02/17/dt1704.xmlC. Booker, 'Substance abuse', *Sunday Telegraph*, 3 March 2002, http://www.telegraph.co.uk/news/uknews/1386576/Christopher-Booker%27s-Notebook.html

C. Booker, 'Asbestos claims on trial', *Sunday Telegraph*, 21 April 2002, http://www.telegraph.co.uk/news/uknews/1391639/Christopher-Booker%27s-Notebook.html

C. Booker, 'Asbestos scare costs homeowners millions', *Sunday Telegraph*, 19 May 2002, http://www.telegraph.co.uk/news/uknews/1394644/Christopher-Booker%27s-Notebook.html

C. Booker, 'Scaremongers cost industry billions', *Sunday Telegraph*, 30 June 2002, http://www.telegraph.co.uk/news/uknews/1398805/Christopher-Booker%27s-Notebook.html

C. Booker, 'No ceiling to the asbestos scam', *Sunday Telegraph*, 18 August 2002, http://www.telegraph.co.uk/news/uknews/1404693/Christopher-Booker%27s-Notebook.html

'Investigation of chrysotile fibres in an asbestos cement', Health and Safety Executive website, undated, http://www.hse.gov.uk/asbestos/issues.htm

C. Booker, 'Tories challenge "sneaky" asbestos legislation', *Sunday Telegraph*, 25 August 2002, http://www.telegraph.co.uk/news/uknews/1405310/Christopher-Booker%27s-Notebook.html

C. Booker, 'Our costliest law must wait', *Sunday Telegraph*, 8 September 2002,
http://www.telegraph.co.uk/news/uknews/1406611/Christopher-Booker%27s-notebook.html

C. Booker, 'The $350bn scam', *Sunday Telegraph*, 15 September 2002,
http://www.telegraph.co.uk/news/uknews/1407234/Christopher-Booker%27s-Notebook.html

C. Booker, 'We put the brake on the costliest law in British history', *Sunday Telegraph*, 20 October 2002, http://www.telegraph.co.uk/news/uknews/1410696/Christopher-Booker%27s-Notebook.html

C. Booker, 'Commons drubbing fails to stop our costliest statute', *Sunday Telegraph*, 27 October 2002, http://www.telegraph.co.uk/news/uknews/1411381/Christopher-Booker%27s-Notebook.html

P. Bodsworth, 'No confusion over law', Letters, *Sunday Telegraph*, 27 October 2002,
http://www.telegraph.co.uk/opinion/main.jhtml?xml=/opinion/2002/10/27/dt2709.xmlC. Booker, 'A blast from Burchill', *Sunday Telegraph*, 10 November 2002,
http://www.telegraph.co.uk/news/worldnews/europe/1412709/Christopher-Booker%27s-Notebook.html

J. Burchill, 'The filthy truth about asbestos', *Guardian*, 2 November 2002,
http://www.guardian.co.uk/Columnists/Column/0,5673,823540,00.html

C. Booker, 'Smallholders lumbered with petty regulation', *Sunday Telegraph*, 17 November 2002,
http://www.telegraph.co.uk/news/uknews/1413403/Christopher-Booker%27s-Notebook.html

C. Booker, 'HSE blunders in new law', *Sunday Telegraph*, 7 December 2002,
http://www.telegraph.co.uk/news/uknews/1415521/Christopher-Booker%27s-Notebook.html

C. Booker, 'How much longer will the HSE tolerate this

racket?', *Sunday Telegraph*, 16 February 2003,
http://www.telegraph.co.uk/news/uknews/1422214/Christopher-
Booker%27s-Notebook.html

C. Booker, 'Home "written off" in mix-up over asbestos',
Sunday Telegraph, 9 November 2003,
http://www.telegraph.co.uk/news/uknews/1446248/Christopher-
Booker%27s-notebook.html

C. Booker, 'The BBC helps to sex up the asbestos threat',
Sunday Telegraph, 1 February 2004,
http://www.telegraph.co.uk/news/uknews/1453151/Christopher-
Booker%27s-notebook.html

C. Booker, 'Let's not spend £8bn to get rid of this stuff',
Sunday Telegraph, 16 May 2004,
http://www.telegraph.co.uk/news/uknews/1461994/Christopher-
Booker%27s-Notebook.html

C. Booker, 'Keep the asbestos hysteria flying', *Sunday
Telegraph*, 23 May 2004,
http://www.telegraph.co.uk/news/worldnews/europe/1462582/Chr
istopher-Booker%27s-Notebook.html

C. Booker, 'EC offices get a clean bill of health – for £1bn',
Sunday Telegraph, 8 August 2004,
http://www.telegraph.co.uk/news/worldnews/europe/1468894/Chr
istopher-Booker%27s-notebook.html

C. Booker, 'HSE has second thoughts on asbestos rip-off',
Sunday Telegraph, 13 November 2004,
http://www.telegraph.co.uk/news/uknews/1476559/Notebook.html

C. Brooker, '"Frivolous asbestos claims" are a serious matter
for Names', *Sunday Telegraph*, 20 February 2005 – no longer
available on the *Telegraph*'s website at the time of writing

C. Brooker, 'A dangerous level of asbestos inexpertise', *Sunday
Telegraph*, 10 October 2005,
http://www.telegraph.co.uk/news/uknews/1499690/Christopher-
Booker%27s-notebook.html

C. Booker, 'Fatal cracks appear in asbestos scam as HSE shifts
its ground', *Sunday Telegraph*, 11 December 2005,
http://www.telegraph.co.uk/news/uknews/1505199/Christopher-

Booker%27s-notebook.html

J. Rees, Health and Safety Executive (HSE) deputy chief executive, *HSE Press Office: Putting the record straight*, 15 December 2005,
http://www.hse.gov.uk/press/record/st151205.htm

C. Booker, 'No, Winifred, the "asbestos in the organ" scam is not "very rare"', *Sunday Telegraph*, 15 January 2006,
http://www.telegraph.co.uk/news/uknews/1507831/Christopher-Booker%27s-notebook.html

C. Booker, 'Environment Agency shows its asbestos ignorance', *Sunday Telegraph*, 5 February 2006,
http://www.telegraph.co.uk/news/uknews/1509655/Christopher-Booker's-notebook.html

C. Booker, 'The bizarre death-by-drawing-pin scare', *Sunday Telegraph*, 9 April 2006,
http://www.telegraph.co.uk/news/uknews/1515200/Christopher-Booker%27s-notebook.html

C. Booker, 'The Environment Agency turns a livelihood to rubble', *Sunday Telegraph*, 16 April 2006,
http://www.telegraph.co.uk/news/uknews/1515856/Christopher-Booker%27s-notebook.html

C. Booker, 'The asbestos sting goes on', *Sunday Telegraph*, 25 June 2006,
http://www.telegraph.co.uk/news/uknews/1522213/Christopher-Booker%27s-notebook.html

C. Booker, 'When we are dead and buried we will be hazardous waste', *Sunday Telegraph*, 16 July 2006,
http://www.telegraph.co.uk/news/uknews/1524033/Christopher-Booker%27s-notebook.html

C. Booker, 'Great asbestos scam faces a revenue loss of £½bn a year', *Sunday Telegraph*, 6 August 2006,
http://www.telegraph.co.uk/news/1525683/Christopher-Booker%27s-notebook.html

See also G. Podger, HSE chief executive, 'The *Sunday Telegraph* article: "Great asbestos scam faces a revenue loss of £½bn a year"', from HSE press office, 9 August 2006, http://www.hse.gov.uk/press/record/st060806.htm

See also 'Refuting Industry Claims That Chrysotile Asbestos Is Safe', Mining Watch Canada website, 23 May 2006, http://mining-watch.ca/index.php?/Asbestos_in_Quebec/chrystotilescience,

C. Booker, 'The BBC falls for the asbestos scam', *Sunday Telegraph*, 15 October 2006,
http://www.telegraph.co.uk/news/uknews/1531446/Christopher-Booker%27s-Notebook.html

C. Booker, 'Why would the BBC have a go at the asbestos watchdog?', *Sunday Telegraph*, 21 October 2006, http://www.telegraph.co.uk/news/uknews/1532048/Christopher-Booker%27s-Notebook.html

C. Booker, 'BBC bites watchdog again', *Sunday Telegraph*, 2 December 2006,
http://www.telegraph.co.uk/news/uknews/1535834/EU-orders-an-end-to-the-Spanish-acquisition.html

2 C. Booker, 'Billions to be spent on nonexistent risk', *Sunday Telegraph*, 13 January 2002,
http://www.telegraph.co.uk/news/main.jhtml?xml=/news/2002/01/13/nbook13.xml

3 'Bookers [sic] Notebook – *Sunday Telegraph* Jan 13th 2002', archived at http://www.warmwell.com/bookerjan12.html – in what appears to be an archived version of the 13 January 2002 *Sunday Telegraph* article 'Billions to be spent on nonexistent risk', Booker is quoted as saying: 'The one professional expert in Britain who has tried to shout about this is John Bridle, based in south Wales, now UK scientific spokesman for the Asbestos Cement Product Producers Association, covering producers in seventeen countries. What particularly alarms Mr Bridle are the wildly unscientific claims made in the growing number of asbestos-related court cases (he is anxious to advise any firm with an asbestos problem, via jbridle@whiteasbestos.fsnet.co.uk); and even more the new regulations proposed by the HSE, which will require every non-domestic property owner to pay for expensive surveys and monitoring of their premises.'

At the time of writing, however, the version of this article archived at the *Telegraph*'s website did not include this paragraph. The first mention by Booker of John Bridle that I could find on the *Telegraph*'s site came several months later: C. Booker, 'Asbestos scare costs homeowners millions', *Sunday Telegraph*, 19 May 2002,

http://www.telegraph.co.uk/news/uknews/1394644/Christopher-Booker%27s-Notebook.html – 'No one has done more to flag up this scandal than John Bridle, an experienced South Wales surveyor and qualified chemist, who has had top-level meetings with the HSE to warn them of the Frankenstein's monster they are unleashing'.

Of the 36 *Sunday Telegraph* articles I found by Christopher Booker on this issue, at least fifteen (19 May 2002, 18 August 2002, 25 August 2002, 8 September 2002, 16 February 2003, 9 November 2003, 10 October 2005, 11 December 2005, 15 January 2006, 5 February 2006, 16 April 2006, 25 June 2006, 15 October 2006, 21 October 2006 and 2 December 2006) contained a favourable mention of John Bridle. But among these, the only reference I could find to Bridle's asbestos-industry links was from 15 October 2006, and it seems somewhat indirect: 'One leading asbestos company was so alarmed by the practices rife in the industry that it even gave Asbestos Watchdog significant financial backing.' From C. Booker, 'The BBC falls for the asbestos scam', by Christopher Booker, *Sunday Telegraph*, 15 October 2006, http://www.telegraph.co.uk/news/uknews/1531446/Christopher-Booker%27s-Notebook.html

4 C. Booker, 'No ceiling to the asbestos scam', *Sunday Telegraph*, 18 August 2002,
   http://www.telegraph.co.uk/news/uknews/1404693/Christopher-Booker%27s-Notebook.html

5 C. Booker, 'Home "written off" in mix-up over asbestos', *Sunday Telegraph*, 9 November 2003,
   http://www.telegraph.co.uk/news/uknews/1446248/Christopher-Booker%27s-notebook.html

6 C. Booker, 'The BBC falls for the asbestos scam', *Sunday Telegraph*, 15 October 2006,

244

http://www.telegraph.co.uk/news/main.jhtml?xml=/news/2006/10/15/nbook15.xml

7 C. Booker, 'We put the brake on the costliest law in British history', *Sunday Telegraph*, 20 October 2002, http://www.telegraph.co.uk/news/uknews/1410696/Christopher-Booker%27s-Notebook.html – 'The new law results from confusion over different types of asbestos, deliberately fostered by a multimillion-pound lobbying campaign by the two French and Belgian multinational companies that dominate the market in selling asbestos substitutes'.

8 C. Booker, 'Billions to be spent on nonexistent risk', *Sunday Telegraph*, 13 January 2002, http://www.telegraph.co.uk/news/uknews/1381270/Christopher-Booker%27s-Notebook.html

9 C. Booker, 'The BBC falls for the asbestos scam', *Sunday Telegraph,* 15 October 2006, http://www.telegraph.co.uk/news/uknews/1531446/Christopher-Booker%27s-Notebook.html

10 See C. Booker, 'We put the brake on the costliest law in British history', *Sunday Telegraph,* 20 October 2002, http://www.telegraph.co.uk/news/uknews/1410696/Christopher-Booker%27s-Notebook.html – 'After investigation of several hundred such claims by an independent expert, readers of this column have in recent months been saved nearly £1 million'.

C. Booker, 'How much longer will the HSE tolerate this racket?', *Sunday Telegraph,* 16 February 2003, http://www.telegraph.co.uk/news/uknews/1422214/Christopher-Booker%27s-Notebook.html – 'Thanks to advice from the asbestos expert John Bridle, the surveyor who has been the chief whistleblower on this racket, readers have been saved nearly £2 million …'

C. Booker, 'Home "written off" in mix-up over asbestos', *Sunday Telegraph,* 9 November 2003, http://www.telegraph.co.uk/news/uknews/1446248/Christopher-Booker%27s-notebook.html – 'Last year, when I highlighted examples of absurd overcharging by ARCA members, this led to three Parliamentary debates (and incidentally saved Sunday Telegraph readers some 3 million pounds)'.

C. Booker, 'A dangerous level of asbestos inexpertise', *Sunday Telegraph,* 10 October 2005, http://www.telegraph.co.uk/news/uknews/1499690/Christopher-Booker%27s-notebook.html – 'This body, run by a genuine asbestos expert, John Bridle, was set up following this column's exposure of how many surveyors and contractors are exploiting the confusion over the dangers of asbestos, and it has saved our readers millions of pounds'.

11 *Hansard Index,* 24 October 2002, columns 496–7, http://www.publications.parliament.uk/pa/cm200102/cmhansrd/vo021024/debtext/21024-30.htm – speaking in a parliamentary debate on white asbestos regulation, the Conservative MP John Bercow warned that 'Ministers, Labour Members of Parliament and trade unions must take care not to allow themselves to become front men and cheerleaders for what could turn out to be one of the most shameless public rackets of our time'. Bercow claimed that 'the Government are seeking to ram through the House highly detailed and controversial regulations, which hon. Members are not equipped technically to evaluate and upon which, plainly, there is not a scientific consensus', and cited the dissenting views of 'John Bridle, an experienced south Wales surveyor, qualified chemist and unpaid consultant to the Asbestos Cement Product Producers Association'. Christopher Booker later claimed that both he and Bridle had given Bercow 'extensive written and verbal briefings' before the debate – see C. Booker, 'The BBC falls for the asbestos scam', *Sunday Telegraph,* 15 October 2006, http://www.telegraph.co.uk/news/uknews/1531446/Christopher-Booker%27s-Notebook.html

12 C. Booker, 'The BBC falls for the asbestos scam', *Sunday Telegraph,* 15 October 2006, http://www.telegraph.co.uk/news/uknews/1531446/Christopher-Booker%27s-Notebook.html

13 C. Booker, 'Great asbestos scam faces a revenue loss of £½bn a

year', *Sunday Telegraph,* 6 August 2006,
http://www.telegraph.co.uk/news/1525683/Christopher-
Booker%27s-notebook.html

14 *You and Yours,* 'A look at the man behind the campaign', BBC
Radio 4, 18 October 2006, http://www.bbc.co.uk/radio4/youandy-
ours/items/01/2006_42_wed.shtml

15 'Asbestos surveyor found guilty of breaching Trade Descriptions
Act', British Occupational Hygiene Society website, 14 April 2005,
http://www.bohs.org/newsArticle.aspx?newsItem=14

16 At the time of writing, John Bridle's CV no longer appeared on
the Asbestos Watchdog website. But the version as archived in
July 2006 could still be viewed at www.archive.org via this link:
http://web.archive.org/web/20060716140437/http://www.asbestos
watchdog.co.uk/johnbridle.html

17 Garry Burdett's paper for the HSE, investigating Booker's claim
'that asbestos fibres undergo a chemical change when mixed with
cement, which bonds them and coats them with calcium, thus
making them non-respirable', can be read here:
http://www.hse.gov.uk/research/hsl_pdf/2007/hsl0711.pdf

18 The CV claims that 'John has recently been awarded a prestigious
honorary degree in Asbestos Sciences from the Russian Academy
of Sciences ... The Academy reviewed the 300,000 words of
asbestos information John has written ... and after inviting him
to address their conference on asbestos and health in Moscow,
confirmed their intention to make him a professor of the
academy. His new professorship makes him the foremost
authority on asbestos science in the world'. The CV gives a list of
Bridle's 'main clients', to whom, it is claimed, he acts as an
'asbestos consultant'. This list includes the *Sunday Telegraph*, BBC
Radio 4, the Conservative Party Shadow Cabinet and the Vale of
Glamorgan Trading Standards Department. Under 'publications',
it is claimed that Bridle has 'co-written for the Booker notebook'.

19 'Survey finds widespread ignorance of asbestos, cancer link',
Cancer Research UK website, 26 February 2008,
http://info.cancerresearchuk.org/news/archive/newsarchive/2008/f
ebruary/18483013

20 'House of Commons written answers', UK Parliament website, 10 January 2002, http://www.publications.parliament.uk/pa/cm200102/cmhansrd/v o020110/text/20110w12.htm

21 See also 'International Agency for Research on Cancer (IARC) – Summaries & Evaluations', quoted at Inter-Organization Programme for the Sound Management of Chemicals website, 6 February 1998, http://www.inchem.org/documents/iarc/suppl7/asbestos.html

22 See 'Asbestos', *American Cancer Society*, 31 January 2006, http://www.cancer.org/docroot/PED/content/PED_1_3X_Asbestos .asp – 'All four main types of commercially used asbestos, chrysotile, amosite, anthophyllite, and mixtures containing croci-dolite, are associated with an increased risk of lung cancer … mesotheliomas have been observed not only among workers who are occupationally exposed to crocidolite, amosite, and chrysotile, but also among their family members and people living in the neighborhoods surrounding asbestos factories and mines'.

See also 'Asbestos CAS No. 1332-21-4', *Report on carcinogens – eleventh edition*, (US) National Institutes of Health: National Institute of Environmental Health Sciences, National Toxicology Program, http://ntp.niehs.nih.gov/ntp/roc/eleventh/ profiles/s016asbe.pdf – 'Asbestos and all commercial forms of asbestos are *known to be human carcinogens* based on sufficient evidence of carcinogenicity in humans. Studies in humans have demonstrated that exposure to asbestos causes respiratory-tract cancer, pleural and peritoneal mesothelioma (tumors of the membranes lining the chest and abdominal cavities and surrounding internal organs), and other cancers. Case reports and epidemiological studies have found that occupational expo-sure to chrysotile, amosite, anthophyllite, mixtures containing crocidolite, and various complex mixtures of asbestos increases the risk of lung cancer'. See also 'HSE confirms white asbestos remains a threat', *Press Release*, Health and Safety Executive, 5 February 2002, http://www.hse.gov.uk/press/2002/e02010.htm –

Whilst the evidence linking high exposures of chrysotile with cancer is compelling [Rochdale pre-1933 cohort, Quebec miners, animal studies], there is more uncertainty about the degree of risk at much lower levels. However, chysotile remains a category 1 carcinogen [IARC 1977, 1979 and 1982, IPCS, EC].

Although the qualitative difference between the different fibres is very widely accepted in the scientific community, there is no real consensus on the quantification of those differences. A recent study [McDonald et al (2001)] suggested that, on the basis of the quantities of different fibres found in mesothelioma case lungs, approximately 10 per cent of all mesothelioma deaths could be attributable to exposure from white asbestos. However such an estimate is difficult to make with any degree of scientific precision.

The first comprehensive review which attempted to quantify these relative risks was carried out by Hodgson and Darnton. Their paper stated that while the risks from chrysotile were significantly less than those from amosite or crocidolite, they were not negligible. Furthermore, they acknowledged the considerable degree of uncertainty in the quantification of these risks.

23 'HSE confirms white asbestos remains a threat', *Press Release*, Health and Safety Executive, 5 February 2002, http://www.hse.gov.uk/press/2002/e02010.htm

24 'No Consensus on Chrysotile Asbestos', United Nations Environment Programme, 13 October 2006, http://new.unep.org/Documents.Multilingual/Default.asp?DocumentID=486&ArticleID=5385&l=en – 'During the conference, many governments expressed serious concern about the failure to list chrysotile asbestos at this time. The World Health Organisation made a statement reminding participants that chrysotile is a human carcinogen and that at least 90,000 people die every year of asbestos-related diseases such as lung cancer and mesothelioma'.

25 'Environment: Disputes 9; European Communities – Asbestos', World Trade Organisation, undated, http://www.wto.org/english/tratop_e/envir_e/edis09_e.htm –

'Chrysotile asbestos is generally considered to be a highly toxic material, exposure to which poses significant threats to human health (such as asbestosis, lung cancer and mesothelioma)'.

26 J.C MacDonald and A.D. MacDonald, 'Chrysotile, tremolite and carcinogenity', *Annals of Occupational Hygiene,* vol. 41, no. 6, 1997, pp. 699–705,
http://annhyg.oxfordjournals.org/cgi/reprint/41/6/699.pdf

27 'New warning over hidden asbestos', BBC News website, 27 February 2006, http://news.bbc.co.uk/1/hi/uk/4753230.stm

28 'Asbestos scare costs homeowners millions', *Sunday Telegraph,* 19 May 2002, http://www.telegraph.co.uk/news/uknews/1394644/Christopher-Booker%27s-Notebook.html – 'John Bridle, an experienced South Wales surveyor and qualified chemist'

C. Booker, 'No ceiling to the asbestos scam', *Sunday Telegraph,* 18 August 2002,
http://www.telegraph.co.uk/news/uknews/1404693/Christopher-Booker%27s-Notebook.html –'John Bridle, a scientifically-trained surveyor'

C. Booker, 'Tories challenge "sneaky" asbestos legislation', *Sunday Telegraph,* 25 August 2002, http://www.telegraph.co.uk/news/uknews/1405310/Christopher-Booker%27s-Notebook.html – 'a fully-qualified expert, John Bridle'

C. Booker, 'Our costliest law must wait', *Sunday Telegraph,* 8 September 2002,
http://www.telegraph.co.uk/news/uknews/1406611/Christopher-Booker%27s-notebook.html – 'our expert John Bridle'

C. Booker, 'How much longer will the HSE tolerate this racket?', *Sunday Telegraph,* 16 February 2003,
http://www.telegraph.co.uk/news/uknews/1422214/Christopher-Booker%27s-Notebook.html – 'the asbestos expert John Bridle, the surveyor who has been the chief whistleblower on this racket'

C. Booker, 'Home "written off" in mix-up over asbestos', *Sunday Telegraph,* 9 November 2003,
http://www.telegraph.co.uk/news/uknews/1446248/Christopher-Booker%27s-notebook.html – 'one of the country's leading asbestos experts, John Bridle'

C. Booker, 'A dangerous level of asbestos inexpertise', *Sunday Telegraph*, 10 October 2005, http://www.telegraph.co.uk/news/uknews/1499690/Christopher-Booker%27s-notebook.html – 'a genuine asbestos expert, John Bridle'; and 'The judge dismissed most charges, but found Mr Bridle guilty of the minor technical offence of using "P402" on a single letter (to the BOHS). Since then the BOHS has lost no opportunity to publicise his conviction. The HSE, well aware of Mr Bridle's expertise, knows better, and now fully supports what Asbestos Watchdog is doing'.

C. Booker, 'Fatal cracks appear in asbestos scam as HSE shifts its ground', *Sunday Telegraph*, 11 December 2005, http://www.telegraph.co.uk/news/uknews/1505199/Christopher-Booker%27s-notebook.html – 'The expert who has done more than anyone to expose this absurdity is John Bridle. The value of his work was recently recognised when he was made an honorary professor by the Russian Occupational Health Institute, part of the Russian Academy of Sciences.'; and 'When Prof. Bridle began to expose the scientific flaws in the regulation of asbestos he was in direct conflict with the HSE. But his marshalling of the evidence, backed by an array of top scientists, has been so authoritative that he and the HSE are now closely collaborating'.

C. Booker, 'No, Winifred, the "asbestos in the organ" scam is not "very rare"', *Sunday Telegraph*, 15 January 2006, http://www.telegraph.co.uk/news/uknews/1507831/Christopher-Booker%27s-notebook.html – 'John Bridle of Asbestos Watchdog, the firm launched through this column to fight the nationwide racket'

C. Booker, 'Environment Agency shows its asbestos ignorance', *Sunday Telegraph*, 5 February 2006, http://www.telegraph.co.uk/news/uknews/1509655/Christopher-Booker%27s-notebook.html – 'Professor John Bridle of Asbestos Watchdog, the firm set up with the aid of this column to puncture the bubble of hysteria surrounding asbestos'

C. Booker, 'The Environment Agency turns a livelihood to rubble', *Sunday Telegraph*, 16 April 2006, http://www.telegraph.co.uk/news/uknews/1515856/Christopher-Booker%27s-notebook.html – 'at this point they were advised to call in Prof John Bridle of Asbestos Watchdog, who is well known to readers of this column'

C. Booker, 'The asbestos sting goes on', *Sunday Telegraph*, 25 June 2006, http://www.telegraph.co.uk/news/uknews/1522213/Christopher-Booker%27s-notebook.html – 'John Bridle, of Asbestos Watchdog (the body set up, with the aid of this column, to combat the scientific and legal confusion that the Asbestos Scam thrives on)'

C. Booker, 'The BBC falls for the asbestos scam', *Sunday Telegraph*, 15 October 2006, http://www.telegraph.co.uk/news/uknews/1531446/Christopher-Booker%27s-Notebook.html – 'a very experienced, knowledgeable and brave whistleblower'; 'Prof John Bridle, Britain's leading practical asbestos expert'

29 C. Booker, 'Keep the asbestos hysteria flying', *Sunday Telegraph*, 23 May 2004, http://www.telegraph.co.uk/news/worldnews/europe/1462582/Christopher-Booker%27sNotebook.html

30 C. Booker, 'Environment Agency shows its asbestos ignorance', *Sunday Telegraph*, 5 February 2006, http://www.telegraph.co.uk/news/uknews/1509655/Christopher-Booker%27s-notebook.html

31 See http://www.publications.parliament.uk/pa/cm200102/cmhansrd/vo021024/debtext/21024-28.htm

32 *You and Yours*, 'A look at the man behind the campaign', BBC Radio 4, 18 October 2006, http://www.bbc.co.uk/radio4/youandyours/items/01/2006_42_wed.shtml

33 C. Booker and R. North, *Scared to Death* (Continuum, 2007).

34 Ibid., chapter 13, p. 319.

35 Ibid., chapter 13, p. 319.

36 Ibid., chapter 13, p. 311.

37 Ibid., chapter 13, p. 276.

38 'About the Institute', *Chrysotile Institute website*, undated, http://www.chrysotile.com/en/about.aspx

39 See http://www.prnewswire.co.uk/cgi/news/release?id=175676

40 'President Participates in Social Security Conversation in New York', Office of the White House Press Secretary website, 24 May 2005, http://www.whitehouse.gov/news/releases/2005/05/20050524-3.html

41 R. Howie, 'Asbestos – Future Risks?', *Environmental and Health International*, vol. 8, no. 1, 2006, p. 17, http://www.ifeh.org/magazine/ifeh-magazine-2006_v8_n1.pdf

42 'Sex, lies and impeachment', BBC News website, 22 December 1998, http://news.bbc.co.uk/1/hi/special_report/1998/12/98/review_of_98/themes/208715.stm

43 C. Whelan, 'Lies, damn lies and politics', *Telegraph*, 24 April 2005, http://www.telegraph.co.uk/arts/main.jhtml?xml=/arts/2005/04/24/boobo224.xml

44 C. Brown, 'Major rounds on Blair over food tax claim', *Independent*, 17 January 1997, http://findarticles.com/p/articles/mi_qn4158/is_19970117/ai_n9643424

45 D. Bartlett, 'Mad cows and democratic governance: BSE and the construction of a 'free market' in the UK', *Crime, Law and Social Change*, vol. 30, no. 3, October 1998, http://www.springerlink.com/content/h6086581q3472183/
    See also S. Dealler, 'At long last, signs of a BSE breakthrough', *Guardian*, 5 September 2001, http://www.guardian.co.uk/uk/2001/sep/05/bse.highereducation
    A. Kirby, 'Ministry "unscientific" over BSE', BBC News website, 21 October 1998, http://news.bbc.co.uk/1/hi/health/background_briefings/bse/197978.stm
    'Consumer groups attack "BSE secrecy"', BBC News website, 28 October 1998, http://news.bbc.co.uk/1/hi/health/background_briefings/bse/203155.stm
    Ministry of Agriculture, Fisheries and Food, 'The BSE Inquiry: The Report', October 2000, vol. 11, chapter 5, October 2000, http://www.bseinquiry.gov.uk/report/volume11/chapter5.htm#480386

46 J. Brignell, '*Scared to Death* book review', Science and Public Policy Institute website, 26 November 2007, http://scienceandpublicpolicy.org/reprint/scaredtodeathreview.html

CHAPTER SIX

1 D. Loravsky, *The Lysenko Affair*, (University of Chicago Press, 1986), p. 59.

2 'Lysenko on the line', Radio Free Europe, 17 December 1957, http://files.osa.ceu.hu/holdings/300/8/3/text/55-1-45.shtml

3 W.B. Gratzer, *The Undergrowth of Science*, (Oxford University Press, 2001), p. 181.

4 'Paperbacks (Review of *Hungry Ghosts* by Jasper Becker)', *Independent*, 23 February 1997, http://findarticles.com/p/articles/mi_qn4158/is_19970223/ai_n14097564

5 Professor H. Sheehan, Dublin City University, 'Who was Lysenko, What was Lysenkoism?', http://webpages.dcu.ie/~sheehanh/lysenko.htm

6 F. Gaglioti, 'The fate of Soviet genetics', World Socialist website, 4 October 1996, http://www.wsws.org/articles/1999/feb1999/sovgen.shtml

7 D. Loravsky, op. cit., p. 211.

8 O.S. Harman, *The Man Who Invented the Chromosome: A Life of Cyril Darlington*, (Harvard University Press, 2004), p. 141.

9 Professor H. Sheehan, Dublin City University, 'Who was Lysenko, What was Lysenkoism?', http://webpages.dcu.ie/~sheehanh/lysenko.htm

10 Z.A. Medvedev, *The Unknown Stalin*, (I.B Tauris, 2006), p. 181.

11 Professor B. Capla, George Mason University, 'Autocratic Ghosts and Chinese Hunger', http://www.gmu.edu/departments/economics/bcaplan/museum/chinhung.htm

12 L. Petrinovich, *The Cannibal within* (Aldine Transaction, 2000), p. 182.

13 'Chinese Famine of 1958–1961', Overpopulation.com website, undated, http://www.overpopulation.com/faq/famine/chinese-famine-of-1958-1961/#footnotes_5

14 J. Shapiro, *Mao's War Against Nature* (Cambridge University Press, 2001), pp. 86–90.

15 F. Watson, 'One hundred years of famine – a pause for reflection',

Emergency Nutrition Network, undated,
http://www.ennonline.net/fex/08/ms20.html

16 Chunhou Zhang and C. Edwin Vaughan, *Mao Zedong as Poet and Revolutionary Leader* (Lexington Books, 2002), pp. 86–7.

17 S.W. Mosher, 'Book Review: *Hungry Ghosts: Mao's Secret Famine* by Jasper Becker', *The Freeman*, December 1997,
http://www.fee.org/Publications/the-Freeman/article.asp?aid=4736

18 N. Eberstadt, 'The Great Leap Backward', *New York Times*, 16 February 1997,
http://www.nytimes.com/books/97/02/16/reviews/970216.16eberst a.html

19 S. Seevak, 'Sakharov, Andrei Dmitryevich', 2003,
http://www.learntoquestion.com/seevak/groups/2003/sites/sakharo v/AS/biography/dissent.html

20 W.B. Gratzer, op. cit., p. 182.

CHAPTER SEVEN

1 Dr Mark Hoofnagle gives a comprehensive 'how to' guide to becoming a denialist crank: M. Hoofnagle, 'Crank HOWTO', Denialism blog, 31 May 2007,
http://scienceblogs.com/denialism/2007/05/crank_howto.php

2 See chapter 4.

3 '911Truth.org – an overview', 911Truth.org website, undated,
http://www.911truth.org/article.php?story=20061014120445472

4 T. Cardy, 'Expert witness says "HIV does not exist"', *Herald Sun*, 19 December 2006,
http://www.news.com.au/heraldsun/story/0,21985,20953506-5005961,00.html

5 'Author Biographies', Institute for Historical Review website, undated, http://www.ihr.org/other/authorbios.html – see also D. Lipstadt, 'Denying the holocaust', *BBC News website*, 1 April 2005,
http://www.bbc.co.uk/history/worldwars/genocide/deniers_01.shtml

6 'Defending the indefensible', *Wall Street Journal*, 24 February 2006, http://online.wsj.com/article/SB114072902656081724-email.html

7 'David Irving – Propagandists' Poster Boy', Anti-Defamation League website, 2001, http://www.adl.org/holocaust/irving.asp

8 'Hitler historian branded a "liar"', BBC News website, 11 January 2000, http://news.bbc.co.uk/1/hi/uk/598044.stm

9 'The ruling against David Irving', *Guardian* website, 11 April 2000, http://www.guardian.co.uk/uk/2000/apr/11/irving1

10 'Irving "unworthy of being called historian"', BBC News website, 10 February 2000, http://news.bbc.co.uk/1/hi/uk/638285.stm

11 http://www.fpp.co.uk/Legal/Penguin/transcripts/day016.htm

12 See chapter 3.

13 A.M. Brandt, *The Cigarette Century,* op. cit., chapter 6, p. 185.

14 'Historians Respond: Denial Denounced as Academic Fraud', Anti-Defamation League website, undated, http://www.adl.org/holocaust/academic.asp

15 'Turk convicted of genocide denial', Al Jazeera website, March 2007, http://english.aljazeera.net/NR/exeres/076A4B0D-1C4E-465B-B22E-F83B57B23878.htm

16 C. McGreal, 'Genocide, what genocide?', *Guardian*, 20 March 2000, http://www.guardian.co.uk/comment/story/0,,181819,00.html

17 G. Monbiot, 'The denial industry', *Guardian,* 19 September 2006, http://www.guardian.co.uk/environment/2006/sep/19/ethical-living.g2

18 A. Beam, 'Just the facts – and they're always right', *Boston Globe,* 4 June 2007, http://www.boston.com/news/globe/living/articles/2007/06/04/just_the_facts____and_theyre_always_right/

19 'Re: Apocalypse of the Psychopaths (Courts free and condemn for Holohoax truth)', Libertyforum website, November 2007, http://www.libertyforum.org/showflat.php?Cat=&Board=news_arts&Number=295557539&page=0&view=collapsed&sb=5&o=21&part=127

20 B. O'Neill, 'Meet the no planers', *New Statesman*, 11 September 2006, http://www.newstatesman.com/200609110028

21 'Was 9/11 a holographic projection?', Chemtrail Central Forum, 28 November 2003, http://www.chemtrailcentral.com/ubb/Forum6/HTML/001633.html

CHAPTER EIGHT

1 F. Chalk, 'After the genocide and the way forward', *International Development Research Centre*, 2007, http://www.idrc.ca/en/ev-108300-201-1-DO_TOPIC.html

2 The French government admitted responsibility days after the arrest of several of their agents in New Zealand – see http://www.guardian.co.uk/politics/2005/aug/23/uk.freedomofinformation

3 An investigation by a senior British police officer, Sir John Stevens, concluded in 2003 that UK forces had 'colluded in dozens of murders' – see http://www.guardian.co.uk/uk/2003/apr/17/northernireland.northernireland2

4 'Enron scandal at-a-glance', BBC News website, 22 August 2002, http://news.bbc.co.uk/1/hi/business/1780075.stm

5 M. Harwood, 'A prayer for the prey', *Guardian* Comment is Free website, 15 April 2008, http://commentisfree.guardian.co.uk/matthew_harwood/2008/04/a_prayer_for_the_prey.html

6 'Factfinding Commission releases video of genocide in Laos', 24 January 2003, http://www.factfinding.org/Past_News_Releases/page23.html

7 A. Perrin, 'Welcome to the jungle', *Time* magazine, 28 April 2003, http://www.time.com/time/magazine/article/0,9171,501030505-447253,00.html

8 'Guy Fawkes', The Gunpowder Plot Society website, undated, http://www.gunpowder-plot.org/fawkes.asp

9 'The Pharmaceutical Drug Cartel Launches World War III To Prevent the Construction of a Healthy World', Dr. Rath Health Foundation website, 13 May 2005, http://www4.dr-rath-foundation.org/open_letters/img-nyt0506/speech_drrath.htm

10 Ibid.

11 M. Rothschild, 'Enough of the 9/11 Conspiracies, Already', Common Dreams website, 12 September 2006, http://www.commondreams.org/views06/0912-20.htm

12 G. Monbiot, 'A 9/11 conspiracy virus is sweeping the world, but it has no basis in fact', 6 February 2007, http://www.guardian.co.uk/commentisfree/2007/feb/06/comment.film

13 M. Rothschild, 'Enough of the 9/11 Conspiracies, Already', Common Dreams website, 12 September 2006, http://www.commondreams.org/views06/0912-20.htm

14 R. North, 'Conspiracy theorists', 1 January 2006, http://rachel-northlondon.blogspot.com/2006/01/conspiracy-theorists.html

15 R. North, 'Jon Ronson: R4', 13 June 2007, http://rachel-northlondon.blogspot.com/2007/06/jon-ronson-r4.html

16 'Brains in vats and the evil demon', *The Matrix* website, undated, http://whatisthematrix.warnerbros.com/rl_cmp/new_phil_brain.html

17 J. Malvern, 'Ex-spook takes on Icke's mantle', *The Times*, 7 August 2007,
    http://www.timesonline.co.uk/tol/news/uk/article2211116.ece

18 http://www.daveshayler.com – see also 'I'm God, says renegade spy David Shayler', *Evening Standard*, 9 August 2007, http://www.thisislondon.co.uk/news/article-23407806-details/I'm+God,+says+renegade+spy+David+Shayler/article.do – see also 'The Messiah is to hold a press conference this week', Conspiraloony Central website, 12 September 2007, http://conspiraloon.blogspot.com/2007/09/messiah-is-to-hold-press-conference.html

19 'The controlled demolition of David Shayler', Famous for 15 Megapixels blog,10 August 2007, http://stefzucconi.blogspot.com/2007/08/controlled-demolition-of-david-shayler.html

20 Foreign and Commonwealth Office 'Iraq's Weapons of Mass Destruction: The Assessment of the British Government', September 2002, http://www.fco.gov.uk/Files/kfile/iraqdossier.pdf – see also: Office of the Prime Minister 'Iraq: Its Infrastructure of Concealment, Deception and Intimidation', March 2003, http://www.pm.gov.uk/files/pdf/Iraq.pdf

21 C. Ames, 'Britain's WMD sleight of hand', *Guardian* Comment is

Free website, 31 January 2008,
http://commentisfree.guardian.co.uk/chris_ames/2008/01/britains
_wmd_sleight_of_hand.html

22 B. Johnson, 'The BBC was doing its job – bring back Gilligan',
Telegraph, 29 January 2004,
http://www.telegraph.co.uk/opinion/main.jhtml?xml=/opinion/20
04/01/29/do2902.xml&sSheet=/opinion/2004/01/29/ixopinion.ht
ml

23 'Saddam braced for "holy war"', *BBC News* website, 25 December
2002,
http://news.bbc.co.uk/1/low/world/middle_east/2604779.stm – see
also T. Harnden, 'Syria now top US target for "regime change"',
Telegraph, 8 April 2003,
http://www.telegraph.co.uk/news/main.jhtml?xml=/news/2003/04/
08/wsyria08.xml&sSheet=/portal/2003/04/08/ixportal.html

24 R. Cohen, 'Rumsfeld is correct – the truth will get out', *New York
Times*, 7 June 2006,
http://select.nytimes.com/iht/2006/06/07/world/IHT07globalist.ht
ml?_r=1&oref=slogin

25 J. Wilson, 'Roswell declassified', *Popular Mechanics* magazine,
undated, http://www.ufoevidence.org/documents/doc380.htm

26 J. Williams, 'Let there be doubt', *Guardian* Comment is Free
website, 1 November 2007,
http://commentisfree.guardian.co.uk/john_williams/2007/11/let_t
here_be_doubt.html

CHAPTER NINE

1 C. Skelton, 'Revealed – the truth behind the *Space Cadets* lie',
Guardian, 19 December 2005,
http://www.guardian.co.uk/media/2005/dec/19/realitytv.channel4

2 'Spoof show "astronauts" revealed', BBC News website, 7
December 2005,
http://news.bbc.co.uk/1/hi/entertainment/4505956.stm

3 'Space cadets back to earth with a bump', *Daily Mail*, 17
December 2005,

http://www.dailymail.co.uk/pages/live/articles/showbiz/show-
biznews.html?in_article_id=371942&in_page_id=1773

4 http://www.guardian.co.uk/media/2005/dec/19/realitytv.channel4

5 Some have suggested that the whole programme might have been
a double-bluff, with all the contestants in on the hoax from the
start and the true deception being played on us, the public.
While no evidence has yet emerged to substantiate this theory,
given the stated aim of this book it would seem unwise to
dismiss the possibility entirely.

6 J. Schwarz and M.L. Wald, 'The Nation: NASA's Curse?;
"Groupthink" Is 30 Years Old, And Still Going Strong', New York
Times, 9 March 2003,
http://query.nytimes.com/gst/fullpage.html?res=9403E5DD1E3FF
93AA35750C0A9659C8B63

7 G. Moorhead, R. Ference and C.P. Neck, 'Group decision fiascos
continue: Space shuttle Challenger and a revised groupthink
framework', Human Relations, vol. 44, no. 6, 1991.

8 Ibid.

9 J. Noble Wilford, 'Shuttle crash: where clues have led so far', New
York Times, 25 February 1986, http://query.nytimes.com/gst/full-
page.html?res=9A0DEFDC103DF936A15751C0A960948260&sec=
health&spon=&pagewanted=2

10 K. Day Lassila, 'A brief history of groupthink', Yale Alumni
Magazine, January/February 2008, http://www.yalealumn-
imagazine.com/issues/2008_01/groupthink.html

11 J.G. Blight and J.M. Lang, The Fog Of War: Lessons From The Life
Of Robert S. McNamara (Rowman and Littlefield, 2005), p. 147.

12 'Bay of Pigs revisited – lessons from a failure', Time magazine, 30
July 1965,
http://www.time.com/time/magazine/article/0,9171,834040-
4,00.html

13 'How Castro humbled Uncle Sam and secured his position as
Cuba's master for 50 years', Daily Mail, 22 February 2008,
http://www.dailymail.co.uk/pages/live/articles/news/worldnews.ht
ml?in_article_id=517645&in_page_id=1811

14 'JFK in History: The Bay of Pigs', John F. Kennedy Presidential

Library and Museum, undated,
http://www.jfklibrary.org/Historical+Resources/JFK+in+History/J
FK+and+the+Bay+of+Pigs.htm

15 I. Janis, 'Groupthink', *Psychology Today*, November 1971, repro-
duced in H.J. Leavitt, L.R. Pondy and D.M. Boje, *Readers in
Managerial Psychology* (University of Chicago Press, 1989).

16 J. Williams and T. Curtis, Unit 3, *Marketing Management in
Practice* (Butterworth-Heinemann, 2006), unit 3, pp. 99–100.

17 A.M. Schlesinger, *A Thousand Days: John F. Kennedy in the White
House* (Houghton Mifflin, 2002 edition), p. 255.

18 B. Barron, 'Vietnam revisited', BBC News website, 16 November
2000, http://news.bbc.co.uk/1/hi/world/asia-pacific/716609.stm

CHAPTER TEN

1 S. Cousseau, 'Lust for Life: My leap of faith', *Continuum* magazine, vol. 5, no. 3, spring 1998, http://www.garynull.com/docu-
ments/Continuum/LustForLifeLeapOfFaith.htm

2 D. Rasnick, 'The Aids Blunder', *Mail and Guardian* (South
Africa), 24 January 2001,
http://www.virusmyth.com/aids/hiv/drblunder.htm

3 C. Schmidt, 'The Group-Fantasy Origins of Aids', *The Journal of
Psychohistory,* summer 1984,
http://www.virusmyth.com/aids/hiv/csfantasy.htm

4 J-E. Robinet, 'Aids And Art: A history of a disease and the arts
campaign to stop it', *Carnegie* magazine, winter 2005,
http://www.carnegiemuseums.org/cmag/bk_issue/2005/winter/feat
ure3.html

5 P. Brown, 'AZT and Aids – The doubts persist', *New Scientist*, 26
October 1991,
http://www.newscientist.com/article/mg13217922.600-azt-and-
aids-the-doubts-persist—us-authorities-have-justlicensed-a-
second-drug-called-ddi-for-the-fight-against-aids-but-medicalscie
ntists—are-still-concerned-over-the-value-of-the-original-drug-
.html

6 'United States Aids cases and deaths by year', AVERT (UK Aids

charity) website, last updated 7 February 2008,
http://www.avert.org/usastaty.htm

7 'Aids Monolith', UK National Archives, undated,
http://www.nationalarchives.gov.uk/films/1979to2006/filmpage_ai
ds.htm

8 'The Duesberg Phenomenon', *Science*, vol. 266, 9 December 1994,
http://www.sciencemag.org/feature/data/cohen/266-5191-
1642a.pdf

9 J. Lauritsen, 'AZT on trial', *New York Native*, 19 October 1987,
http://www.virusmyth.com/aids/hiv/jltrial.htm

10 American Psychiatric Association, 'Gay, Lesbian and Bisexual
Issues', undated, http://www.healthyminds.org/glbissues.cfm

11 'Poison by Prescription' (overview), Reviewing Aids website,
undated,
http://www.reviewingaids.org/awiki/index.php/Poison_by_Prescri
ption

12 'The group', Virusmyth website, undated,
http://www.virusmyth.com/aids/group.htm

13 C. Farber, 'Fatal Distraction', *Spin* magazine, June 1992,
http://www.virusmyth.com/aids/hiv/cffatal.htm

14 'Bookshelf' (overview of John Lauritsen's *The AIDS War:
Propaganda, profiteering and genocide from the medical-industrial
complex*), Virusmyth website, undated,
http://www.virusmyth.com/aids/books/jlbwar.htm

15 N. Hodgkinson, 'Conspiracy of Silence', *Sunday Times*, 3 April
1994,
http://www.reviewingaids.org/awiki/index.php/Document:Conspir
acy_of_Silence

16 'The Duesberg Phenomenon', *Science*, vol. 266, 9 December 1994,
http://www.sciencemag.org/feature/data/cohen/266-5191-
1642a.pdf

17 Schechter et al, 'HIV-1 and the aetiology of Aids', *The Lancet*,
March 1993,
http://www.ncbi.nlm.nih.gov/pubmed/8095571?dopt=Abstract –
see also 'The Evidence That HIV Causes Aids', US National
Institute of Allergy and Infectious Diseases website, last updated

27 February 2003, http://www.niaid.nih.gov/Factsheets/
evidhiv.htm

18 'Unexplained opportunistic infections and CD4+ T-lymphocytopenia without HIV infection. An investigation of cases in the
United States. The Centers for Disease Control Idiopathic CD4+
T-lymphocytopenia Task Force', *New England Journal of Medicine*,
vol. 328, no. 6, 11 February 1993,
http://content.nejm.org/cgi/content/abstract/328/6/373

19 'Peter Duesberg, Bird Flu Flop, and How to Heal on RSBell Radio',
RSBell Radio (online), 18 March 2006,
http://www.rsbell.com/radio/modules.php?name=News&file=article
&sid=418 – see also 'David Crowe challenges physics professor
Randall Scalise to invite a dissident instead of just dissing them.
And then Randi the Magician gets involved ...', Rethinking Aids
website, last updated 16 March 2008,
http://www.rethinkingaids.com/challenges/Crowe-Scalise-et-al.html

20 B. Radford, 'The flawed guide to Bigfoot', *Skeptical Inquirer*
magazine, January/February 2000, http://www.csicop.org/si/2000-
01/bigfoot.html

21 N. Hodgkinson, 'The Cure That Failed', 4 April 1993,
http://www.duesberg.com/articles/nhcure.html

22 'Death of an HIV dissident', email from Paul Blanchard, archived
at Aids info BBS online database, dated 9 September 1995,
http://www.aidsinfobbs.org/articles/quilty/q03/1344 – see also
'Aids denialists who have died', Aidstruth.org website, undated,
http://www.aidstruth.org/aids-denialists-who-have-died.php

23 'United States Aids cases and deaths by year', AVERT website, last
updated 7 February 2008, http://www.avert.org/usastaty.htm

24 http://www.altheal.org/continuum/continuum.htm – accessed 3
November 2007

25 M. Baumgartner, 'In Memoriam – Huw Christie Harry Williams
– 9 February 1960–17 August 2001', October 2001,
http://www.virusmyth.com/aids/hiv/mbobituaryhc.htm

26 J. Kirkham and L. Scheff, 'Mark Griffiths Memorial', Altheal
website, undated,
http://www.altheal.org/altheal/markmemorial.htm

27 G. Cairns, 'Despair, Dissidence, Defiance', *Positive Nation* online,
    issue 82, July/August 2002,
    http://www.positivenation.co.uk/issue80_81/features/feature1/feat
    ure1_2.htm

28 'HIV and Aids', Aids Truth website, undated,
    http://www.aidstruth.org/

29 D. Rasnick, 'The Aids Blunder', *Mail and Guardian* (South
    Africa), 24 January 2001,
    http://www.virusmyth.com/aids/hiv/drblunder.htm

30 http://www.virusmyth.com/aids/books/jlbrevwar.htm -
    'Bookshelf', by Mike Chappelle, January/February 1994

31 J. Lauritsen, 'Aids – a Death Cult', Communication Agents Initiative
    website, 13 September 2004, http://www.communicationagents.
    com/emma_holister/2004/09/13/aids_a_death_cult_by.htm

32 I. Young, 'Cocktails for one – Aids treatment as a social
    sacrament', HIV Realist website, December 1998,
    http://www.virusmyth.com/aids/hiv/iycocktails.htm

33 T. Mbeki, 'Thabo Mbeki's letter', PBS News website, 3 April 2000,
    http://www.pbs.org/wgbh/pages/frontline/aids/docs/mbeki.html

CHAPTER ELEVEN

1 J. Myburgh, 'The Virodene Affair – I – The secret history of the
   ANC's response to the HIV/Aids epidemic', Politicsweb website,
   17 September 2007,
   http://www.politicsweb.co.za/politicsweb/view/politicsweb/en/page
   71619?oid=83156&sn=Detail

2 Ibid.

3 C. Platt, 'Hearts, brains and minds', Cryonet website, undated,
   http://www.cryocare.org/index.cgi?subdir=ccrpt10&url=visser.html

4 J. Myburgh, 'The Virodene Affair – III – How the MCC was
   eventually taken out; and why Virodene was nonetheless still
   banned in SA', Politicsweb website, 18 September 2007,
   http://www.politicsweb.co.za/politicsweb/view/politicsweb/en/page
   71619?oid=83213&sn=Detail

5 'World: Africa Apartheid government sought germs to kill blacks',

BBC News website, 12 June 1998,
http://news.bbc.co.uk/1/hi/world/africa/110947.stm

6 C. Paton, 'Save our babies, Dr Zuma; Decision against drug treatment puts thousands of infants at risk', *Sunday Times of South
   Africa*, 11 October 1998,
   http://www.aegis.org/news/suntimes/1998/ST981002.html

7 'AZT: A medicine from hell', archived at Aids Info BBS database,
   dated 17 March 1999,
   http://www.aidsinfobbs.org/debate.html#Brinkstatement – see
   also 'A Democratic Alliance Public Health Warning! – South
   Africa's top twelve Aids dissidents', Democratic Alliance website,
   undated,
   http://www.da.org.za/DA/Site/Eng/campaigns/DOCS/Top12AidsD
   issidents_Combined.doc

8 R.L. Swarns, 'Safety of Common Aids Drug Questioned in South
   Africa', *New York Times*, 25 November 1999,
   http://query.nytimes.com/gst/fullpage.html?res=9E07E3DC163FF9
   36A15752C1A96F958260

9 M. Schoofs, 'Flirting With Pseudoscience', *Village Voice*, 14 March
   2000,
   http://www.villagevoice.com/news/0011,schoofs,13263,1.html

10 P. Salopek, 'South Africa lends ear to Aids sceptics', *Chicago
   Tribune*, 14 April 2000,
   http://www.aegis.com/news/ct/2000/CT000402.html

11 N. Hodgkinson, 'Some observers are critical of HIV theory and
   they have a right to be heard', *Sunday Independent*
   (Johannesburg) 9 July 2000,
   http://www.reviewingaids.org/awiki/index.php/Document:Observ
   ers_Are_Critical

12 H. Christie, 'Suspend all HIV testing ... Mbeki expert panel
   recommends', *New African,* September 2000,
   http://findarticles.com/p/articles/mi_qa5391/is_200009/ai_n21459
   783/pg_1

13 C. Farber, 'Aids and South Africa – a contrary conference in
   Pretoria', *New York Press*, 25 May 2000,
   http://www.virusmyth.com/aids/hiv/cfmbeki.htm

14 http://www.globalpolicy.org/socecon/tncs/pharms1.htm

15 L. Altenroxel, 'Aids panel's report reveals divergent views', *Independent Online*, 4 April 2001, http://www.iol.co.za/general/newsview.php?click_id=125&art_id= ct20010404201008215A3261683&set_id=1

16 'Don't call me Manto', BBC News website, 14 September 2000, http://news.bbc.co.uk/1/hi/world/africa/924889.stm

17 'Aids in South Africa – treatment, transmission and the government', AVERT website, last updated 11 March 2008, http://www.avert.org/aids-south-africa.htm

18 'Mbeki accuses CIA over Aids', BBC News website, 6 October 2000, http://news.bbc.co.uk/1/hi/world/africa/959579.stm

19 'Questions over death of Mbeki aide', BBC News website, 27 October 2000, http://news.bbc.co.uk/1/hi/world/africa/994505.stm

20 J. Myburgh, 'The Virodene Affair – V – How the efficacy of Virodene was finally put to the test, and why the war on anti-retrovirals ended', Politicsweb website, 18 September 2007, http://www.politicsweb.co.za/politicsweb/view/politicsweb/en/page 71619?oid=83253&sn=Detail

21 T. Mbeki, 'Address by President Thabo Mbeki at the Inaugural ZK Matthews Memorial Lecture', 12 October 2001, http://www.anc.org.za/ancdocs/history/mbeki/2001/tm1012.html

22 'Court orders South Africa to treat pregnant HIV-positive women with nevirapine', *Bulletin of the World Health Organisation*, vol. 80, 2002, http://www.scielosp.org/scielo.php?script=sci_arttext&pid=S0042-96862002000400019&lng=e&nrm=iso&tlng=e

23 S. Power, 'The Aids rebel', *The New Yorker*, May 2003, http://www.pbs.org/pov/pov2003/stateofdenial/special_rebel4.html

24 'Official nod for voodoo trials?', *Mail and Guardian* (South Africa), 28 October 2005, http://www.mg.co.za/articlePage.aspx?articleid=255040&area=/ins ight/insight__comment_and_analysis/

25 'The Pharmaceutical Drug Cartel Launches World War III To Prevent the Construction of a Healthy World', Dr. Rath Health Foundation website, 13 May 2005, http://www4.dr-rath-

foundation.org/open_letters/img-nyt0506/speech_drrath.htm

26 N. Nattrass, *Mortal Combat – Aids Denialism and the Struggle for Antiretrovirals in South Africa* (University of KwaZulu-Natal Press, 2007), p. 138.

27 Unknown authors, 'Castro Hlongwane, Caravans, Cats, Geese, Foot & Mouth and Statistics – HIV/Aids and the Struggle for the Humanisation of the African', March 2002, http://www.virusmyth. com/aids/hiv/ancdoc.htm

28 Extracts from P. Feyerabend, *Against Method – Outline of an anarchistic theory of knowledge* (Humanities Press, 1975), http://www.marxists.org/reference/subject/philosophy/works/ge/fe yerabe.htm

29 A. Brink, 'Debating AZT – Mbeki and the Aids drug controversy', November 2000, http://www.altheal.org/toxicity/debazt.htm

30 G. Johnson, 'Bright Scientists, Dim Notions', *New York Times*, 28 October 2007, http://www.nytimes.com/2007/10/28/weekinre-view/28johnson.html?_r=1&ex=1194321600&en=719248bb5a1ca0 f4&ei=5070&oref=slogin

31 'Foreword to Inventing the Aids virus', Virusmyth website, undated, http://www.virusmyth.com/aids/hiv/kmforeword.htm

32 A. Russel Wallace, 'Vaccination a delusion – Its penal enforce-ment a crime', 1898, http://www.whale.to/vaccine/wallace/comp.html

CHAPTER TWELVE

1 P. Graham, 'What you can't say', undated, http://www.paulgraham.com/say.html

2 A. Maitland, 'Throw the rule-book out of the window', *Financial Times*, 8 February 2000, http://www.paconsulting.com/news/about_pa/2000/about_pa_200 002080.htm

3 B. McLean, 'Is Enron over-priced?', *Fortune* magazine, 5 March 2001, http://money.cnn.com/2006/01/13/news/companies/ enronoriginal_fortune/index.htm

4 'Enron's Chief Executive Quits After Only 6 Months in Job', *New*

York Times, 15 August 2001, http://query.nytimes.com/gst/
fullpage.html?res=9405E0D8163EF936A2575BC0A9679C8B63
5 Ibid.
6 Ibid.
7 S.L. Lang, 'A Market Bubble Bursts When Reality Pierces Hype',
Wall Street Journal,
http://online.wsj.com/article_print/SB1021405451677470880.html
8 Four definitions of 'paradigm' from www.dictionary.com – see
http://dictionary.reference.com/browse/paradigm
9 M. Atkinson, 'Mervyn King mocks paradigm pundits', *Guardian*,
18 May 1999,
http://www.guardian.co.uk/business/1999/may/18/10

CHAPTER THIRTEEN

1 S. Blackburn, 'Does Relativism Matter?', *Butterflies and Wheels*,
http://www.butterfliesandwheels.com/articleprint.php?num=154
2 'Census returns of the Jedi', BBC News website, 13 February
2003, http://news.bbc.co.uk/1/hi/uk/2757067.stm
3 'Jedi "religion" grows in Australia', BBC News website, 27 August
2002, http://news.bbc.co.uk/1/hi/entertainment/2218456.stm
4 Accessed 9 January 2008.
5 R. Dawkins, *The God Delusion* (Bantam Press, 2006), p. 403.
6 Ibid., p. 397.
7 Ibid., p. 347.
8 Comment no. 1044428 on A. Rutherford, 'What if you're wrong?',
Guardian Comment is Free website, 11 January 2008,
http://commentisfree.guardian.co.uk/adam_rutherford/2008/01/w
hat_if_youre_wrong.html#comment-1044428

CHAPTER FOURTEEN

1 A. Sullivan, 'Bush's torturers follow where the Nazis led', *The
Times*, 7 October 2007,

http://www.timesonline.co.uk/tol/comment/columnists/andrew_s
ullivan/article2602564.ece

2   President G.W. Bush, 'Text of Bush's Order on Treatment of
    Detainees', 7 February 2002,
    http://www.kron.com/global/story.asp?s=1962000&ClientType=Pr
    intable

3   'Redefining torture?', PBS News website, 18 October 2005,
    http://www.pbs.org/wgbh/pages/frontline/torture/themes/redefini
    ng.html

4   S. Wilson and S. Chan, 'As Insurgency Grew, So Did Prison
    Abuse', *Washington Post*, 10 May 2004,
    http://www.washingtonpost.com/ac2/wp-dyn/A13065-
    2004May9?language=printer

5   O.G. Davidson, 'The Secret File of Abu Ghraib', *Rolling Stone*
    magazine, 14 July 2005, http://www.rollingstone.com/
    politics/story/6388256/the_secret_file_of_abu_ghraib/
    See also '"The Road to Abu Ghraib", IV. Iraq: Applying Counter-
    Terrorism Tactics during a Military Occupation', Human Rights
    Watch, June 2004,
    http://www.hrw.org/reports/2004/usa0604/5.htm

6   J. White, 'Abu Ghraib Tactics Were First Used at Guantanamo',
    Washington Post, 14 July 2005, http://www.washingtonpost.
    com/wp-dyn/content/article/2005/07/13/AR2005071302380.html

7   D. Jehl and E. Schmitt, 'The Reach of War: The Interrogators;
    Afghan Policies On Questioning Landed in Iraq', *New York Times*,
    21 May 2004, http://query.nytimes.com/gst/fullpage.
    html?res=9F04EFD7113FF932A15756C0A9629C8B63

8   'Abuse of Iraqi POWs by GIs probed', *CBS News*, 28 April 2004,
    http://www.cbsnews.com/stories/2004/04/27/60II/main614063.sht
    ml

9   D. Glaister and J. Borger, '1,800 pictures add to US disgust',
    Guardian, 13 May 2004,
    http://www.guardian.co.uk/world/2004/may/13/iraq.usa

10 'SBS broadcasts Abu Ghraib images', News.com.au website, 15
    February 2006, http://www.news.com.au/story/0,10117,18162096
    29277,00.html

11 'The Road to Abu Ghraib', Human Rights Watch report, June
   2004,
   http://www.hrw.org/reports/2004/usa0604/1.htm#_Toc74483690
12 J. Zhang, 'Prof. Zimbardo faults Rumsfeld for Abu Ghraib', *The
   Stanford Daily*, 29 October 2004,
   http://daily.stanford.edu/article/2004/10/29/profZimbardoFaultsR
   umsfeldForAbuGhraib
13 J.R. Schlesinger, 'Final Report of the Independent Panel to
   Review DoD Detention Operations', 24 August 2004, p. 114 – see
   http://news.bbc.co.uk/nol/shared/bsp/hi/pdfs/24_08_04_abughrai
   breport.pdf
14 Ibid., p. 118.
15 D. Leigh, 'UK forces taught torture methods', *Guardian*, 8 May
   2004,
   http://politics.guardian.co.uk/iraq/story/0,12956,1212199,00.html
16 'U.S. Troops Tortured Iraqis in Mosul, Documents Show',
   Reuters/Common Dreams website, 26 March 2005,
   http://www.commondreams.org/headlines05/0326-01.htm
17 'No Blood, No Foul – Soldiers' Accounts of Detainee Abuse in
   Iraq', Human Rights Watch, July 2006,
   http://www.hrw.org/reports/2006/us0706/2.htm
18 J.H. Richardson, 'Acts of Conscience', *Esquire*, 1 July 2006,
   http://www.esquire.com/features/ESQ0806TERROR_102
19 'The torture question – interview with John Yoo', PBS News, 18
   October 2005 – last updated October 2007,
   http://www.pbs.org/wgbh/pages/frontline/torture/interviews/yoo.h
   tml
20 'Newly Released Army Documents Point to Agreement Between
   Defense Department and CIA on "Ghost" Detainees, ACLU Says',
   American Civil Liberties Union website, 3 October 2005,
   http://www.aclu.org/safefree/general/17597prs20050310.html
21 'US held youngsters at Abu Ghraib', BBC News website, 11 March
   2005, http://news.bbc.co.uk/1/hi/world/americas/4339511.stm
22 G. Orwell, 'Politics and the English Language', 1946,
   http://www.george-orwell.org/Politics_and_the_
   English_Language/0.html

23 V. Pellizzari, 'Kang Khek Ieu: "They all had to be eliminated"', *Independent*, 11 February 2008, http://www.independent.co.uk/news/world/asia/they-all-had-to-be-eliminated-780684.html

24 'Thailand – Not Enough Graves: The War on Drugs, HIV/Aids, and Violations of Human Rights', Human Rights Watch website, July 2004, http://www.hrw.org/reports/2004/thailand0704/1.htm#_Toc76203 861

25 'Full text of Colin Powell's speech', *Guardian*, 5 February 2003, http://www.guardian.co.uk/world/2003/feb/05/iraq.usa2

26 'CIA's harsh interrogation techniques described', ABC News, 18 November 2005, http://abcnews.go.com/WNT/Investigation/story?id=1322866

27 P. Staines (aka Guido Fawkes), 'Suspicious Minds and Convicting Politicians', Guido Fawkes blog, 2 February 2008, http://www.order-order.com/2008/02/suspicious-minds-and-convicting.html

28 M. Foster MP, 'New law protects the right to protest', Letters, *Independent*, 12 December 2005, http://comment.independent.co.uk/letters/article332482.ece

29 C. Murray, 'Damning documentary evidence unveiled. Dissident bloggers in coordinated exposé of UK government lies over torture', Craig Murray's website, 29 December 2005, http://www.craigmurray.org.uk/archives/2005/12/damning_docu men.html

30 Ibid.

31 D. Howarth, 'Who wants the Abolition of Parliament Bill?', *The Times*, 21 February 2006, http://www.timesonline.co.uk/tol/comment/columnists/guest_con tributors/article733022.ece

32 'The Problem', Save Parliament! website, undated, http://www.saveparliament.org.uk/problem.php

CONCLUSION

1 See chapter 1.
2 P. Fray, 'MP tells of Blair's honourable deception', *Sydney Morning Herald*, 19 June 2003, http://www.smh.com.au/articles/2003/06/18/1055828383822.html – see also - C. Ames, 'Britain's WMD sleight of hand', *Guardian* Comment is Free website, 31 January 2008, http://commentis-free.guardian.co.uk/chris_ames/2008/01/britains_wmd_sleight_of_hand.html
3 J. Ungoed-Thomas, 'MPs to be forced to reveal housing claims', *The Times*, 27 February 2008, http://www.timesonline.co.uk/tol/news/politics/article3440819.ece
4 J. Moore, 'À Duesberg, adieu!', *Nature*, vol. 380, 28 March 1996, http://www.aidstruth.org/inventing.php
5 M. Mazzetti, 'Spy agencies say Iraq war worsens terrorism threat', *New York Times*, 24 September 2006, http://www.nytimes.com/2006/09/24/world/middleeast/24terror.html
6 'Ministry of Truth' website, http://www.ministry-of-truth.net/theact.php
7 G. O'Donovan, 'Last night on television', *Telegraph*, 12 October 2007, http://www.telegraph.co.uk/arts/main.jhtml?xml=/arts/2007/10/12/nosplit/bvtv12last.xml

AUTHOR'S NOTE

Credit for this book must ultimately go to Simon Flynn, who conceived the idea and provided much prompt and useful advice while I was realising it. As always, the encouragement and wise words of my agent Louise Greenberg were also indispensible. I'd like to thank Icon's Andrew Furlow and Najma Finlay for their enthusiastic support and good ideas, and Sarah Higgins for her hard work and useful suggestions for improving the text.

While writing the book I had many long conversations with my uncle, James Wilson, and these helped to make it a far more robust piece of work than it would otherwise have been. I also owe an enormous debt to my wife Heleen, who patiently endured many late nights, and much loud enthusiasm.

I'm also grateful to the many friends, colleagues and family members who showed an interest (or at least pretended to, very convincingly), and gave suggestions or feedback – these include Sean, Liz, Jonathan, Amanda, Anthony, Chris, Sue, Gemma, Thommo, Jonah, Dean, Victoria, Ruma, Robert, Mohammad, Kat, Katy, Samina, Amy, Kim, Sara, Natalia, Lara, Tamsin, Volker, David, Jimmy, Symon, Carl, Catherine, and my mother, Margot Wilson.

INDEX